THIRD EDITION

HOW TO BE INVISIBLE

THOMAS DUNNE BOOKS
ST. MARTIN'S PRESS
NEW YORK

THIRD EDITION

HOW TO BE INVISIBLE

PROTECT YOUR HOME,
YOUR CHILDREN,
YOUR ASSETS,
AND YOUR LIFE

J. J. LUNA

This publication is for informational purposes only and should not be used as a substitute for legal or other professional advice. If professional advice or other expert assistance is required, the services of a competent professional should be sought to address the particular circumstances involved.

THOMAS DUNNE BOOKS.
An imprint of St. Martin's Press.

HOW TO BE INVISIBLE: THIRD EDITION. Copyright © 2012 by Editorial de Las Islas LC. All rights reserved. Printed in the United States of America. For information, address St. Martin's Press, 175 Fifth Avenue, New York, N.Y. 10010.

www.thomasdunnebooks.com
www.stmartins.com

Library of Congress Cataloging-in-Publication Data

Luna, J. J.
    How to be invisible : protect your home, your children, your assets, and your life / J. J. Luna.—3rd. ed.
        p. cm.
    ISBN 978-1-250-01045-2 (hardcover)
    ISBN 978-1-250-01515-0 (e-book)
1. Privacy, Right of—United States.   2. Identification—United States.
3. Computer security—United States.   I. Title.
    JC596.2.U5L86 2012
    323.44'80973—dc23

                                                        2012014655

First Edition: July 2012

10 9 8 7 6 5 4 3 2 1

A NOTE TO READERS

This book is dedicated to an anonymous member of Spain's Secret Police. On January 27, 1960, during a brief encounter on a quiet back street in Santa Cruz de Tenerife, I asked him for advice on how best to avoid any problems in the land of Generalissimo Francisco Franco. The advice he gave me has served me well for more than fifty years. He said there was only one way to avoid troubles with the authorities:

"Make yourself invisible."

And so I did.

CONTENTS

PREFACE

What's Changed, and What Stays the Same

In 1997, the basic information you are about to read in chapters 1 through 12 sold for $297. It was called *The Privacy Report* and was sold by mail. When the orders came in—over 300 the first year—I printed the report myself, punched the pages, and inserted them into a three-ring binder. Although I included a two-year money-back guarantee, only 2 percent of the readers asked for a refund—the other 98 percent apparently considered the $297 to be a fair price.

In 1998, I decided to abandon all the mail-order work so my agent sold the report to St. Martin's Press. When it was published in 2000 as *How to Be Invisible*, I was profiled in *Playboy*, quoted in *The Wall Street Journal*, and featured on *The G. Gordon Liddy Show*. The book climbed to number 37 on Amazon.com and stayed high on the list, year after year, as the best-selling book on privacy. A revised edition was published in 2004 but now, eight years later, the time has come for a completely updated international-oriented version that includes information on smartphones, facial recognition, and social networks.

THIRD EDITION

HOW TO BE INVISIBLE

HOW THIS BOOK CAN MAKE YOU INVISIBLE

One day you can be on the top of the world; the next day you can be in hell. One of Wiley Miller's *Non Sequitur* cartoon strips is titled "LEGAL MUGGING." It shows a businessman on the sidewalk of a dark street with his hands in the air. A sign on a post reads:

CAUTION:
WATCH FOR TRIAL ATTORNEYS.

Stepping from a narrow alley is a lawyer wearing a stocking cap, dark glasses, and holding out a legal document.

"This is a frivolous lawsuit," says the attorney to his victim. "You can either spend years and thousands of dollars defending yourself, or we can settle out of court right now."

Although this was in a comic strip, what it portrays is not comical—especially when you are served without a hint of advance warning. More than 1 million lawsuits are filed each year in this country. How many of those do you think are frivolous, but are nevertheless settled out of court?

More than one reader has answered a knock on the door and went into shock at being greeted by reporters, photographers, and trucks with big satellite dishes outside of his or her home! From this day forward, when you read your newspaper or watch the news on TV, start searching for cases where an unknown person is suddenly thrust into the national spotlight, then ask yourself:

COULD THIS POSSIBLY HAPPEN TO ME?

The following are just a few of the many things that could bring the media, or worse, to your home:

- A bomb goes off, you were in the area, and the FBI thinks you fit the profile.
- An identity sketch of the person who robbed the convenience store at 11:45 p.m. last night is flashed on TV, and it looks just like you. And you don't have a plausible excuse for that time that anyone's going to believe.
- You were innocently involved with the wrong people and the 60 Minutes crew is within minutes of tracking you down.
- Someone faked your e-mail address when searching for sex with twelve-year-olds, and the police are at your door.

An article in Newsweek, titled "Getting the Wrong Man," gives a chilling example of something that occurs more often than you might think.

Tom Kennedy found the body of his wife, Irene, who had been strangled and stabbed 29 times while on her daily stroll through a park in the Boston suburb of Walpole. Then, a few hours later, the police called at a nearby dilapidated bungalow where Eddie Burke, a 48-year-old handyman, lived with his mother . . . He was practically a textbook match for police profilers: a loner who knew the victim and was clearly eccentric.

What on earth does "eccentric" mean? My best friends—with a smile—call *me* eccentric. Do I therefore fit a certain profile?

Burke was visibly nervous and gave contradictory answers when questioned by investigators.

Wouldn't you be nervous, too?

There was blood on his clothes and hands. And forensic dentists would soon match his teeth with bite marks left on Mrs. Kennedy's breast.

Burke was arrested for murder. Within twenty-four hours, the police learned that the DNA from the saliva on Mrs. Kennedy's chest could not have come from Burke. Did they then release him?

Incredulously, they ran more tests, which again exonerated him. In addition, blood found on Burke turned out to be feline; he had been tending to injured cats. A palm print left on Mrs. Kennedy's thigh didn't match Burke's hand, while the bite-mark evidence proved inconclusive . . . Yet for six weeks, police kept insisting they had the right man in jail . . . While he was locked away, Burke's life was put under a microscope. He was demonized in newspapers and on TV, each story accompanied by a menacing courtroom image of Burke. The sociopathic profiles were fueled by details of his home's contents—X-rated videotapes, kitchen knives, the book *Men Who Hate Women and the Women Who Love Them*. "They didn't mention the three Bibles in my room," Burke says. "They could just as easily said I was a religious fanatic."

The police claim they followed a logical course and "had the backing of reputed scientific experts." Let us assume that is correct. The point is that even though Burke was the wrong man, *the contents of his house were published by the media.*

Suppose *you* are suddenly arrested, even though innocent of the accused crime, and the contents of your home or personal information are made public? Would anything on the following list—if found in your house—give you cause for concern?

- Excess cash?
- Guns and ammunition?
- The contents of your smartphone?
- All the e-mails you've ever sent or received?
- Empty whiskey bottles or evidence of substance abuse?
- Statements from your bank, your broker, your credit card company?
- The contents on your computer's hard drive, including so-called deleted files, along with a list of every search you've ever made on Google?

If the police are after you, whether you are guilty or not, what is your first priority? Is it not *time*?

You need *time* to think, *time* to get certain items out of the house, *time* to locate your attorney, or—heaven forbid—*time* to pick up some cash, arrange transportation, and flee. This book is designed to give you that time, and to help you keep your private information *private*.

Before we continue, let me say that if someone with *unlimited funds* is after you, you will eventually be found. If you doubt this, contact a competent private investigator and say, "I wish to disappear so completely that even *you* couldn't find me. Can you help me?" The six-word answer will be, "No, because I can find anyone!"

And I agree. Repeatedly, private investigators (PIs) make this point in their books, articles, and personal interviews. And if the police are truly after you, *their* record isn't bad, either. Captain

Robert L. Snow, a police officer for more than twenty-five years, says in his book *Protecting Your Life, Home, and Property* that the Indianapolis Police Department finds 98 or 99 percent of all persons reported to them as missing.

In the Private Investigator section of my home library, I find no PIs anywhere who will admit defeat under any circumstances, *as long as payment is forthcoming.* The closest I can come to a failure is a certain PI who says he successfully tracked down 298 of the 299 targets he was given over his lifetime. As for the one he missed, he eventually concluded that he was given false information, and that no such person ever existed.

The fuel that runs a private investigator's engine is M-O-N-E-Y. In your present situation, a PI may come up with your home address with a single phone call, and with a list of your assets the next day. Where this book can help you, then, is to:

1. Plug the immediate loopholes in your security.
2. Put you on guard, before you ever again give out your Social Security number, home address, or correct date of birth, to anyone other than a government agency.
3. Make it so expensive to trace you and/or your assets that the bad guys or gals will give up before achieving their goals.

THE FOUR LEVELS OF PRIVACY

The direct correlation between money and results cannot be overemphasized. In the sections to come, I'll be referring to various levels of security, with a general outline as follows. However, there may be no clear-cut divisions between one level and the next—it depends on who is after you, why, and the price he or she is willing to pay.

LEVEL ONE

Very basic, economical moves that will give you more privacy than 98 percent of the general population. The opposition might have to pay a private investigator several hundred dollars to track you down.

LEVEL TWO

At this point your utilities, your smartphones, and your other electronic devices will be in alternate names. The license plates on your vehicles will not reveal your true name and address. Anything confidential will be shredded. The PI may now require $5,000 or more in order to track you down.

LEVEL THREE

This will almost certainly require a move from your present location. Both your home (or rental property) and your vehicles will be in the names of anonymous limited liability companies (LLCs). Your home address will now be hidden from all but your closest relatives and friends. It will no longer appear on your annual tax returns, *or anywhere else*. If you follow the directions in chapter 12, "E-mail and the Internet," your Internet/e-mail connections will be under cover and the black-hat boys and/or the law firms may have to pay a PI some truly serious money to track you down. Are you worth that much to them? If not, sleep well.

LEVEL FOUR

At this level you are duplicating the federal Witness Security Program (incorrectly called the Witness "Protection" Program in the media) for criminals protected by the U.S. government. When the Feds do it for a felon, it's legal. When you do it for yourself, it's illegal.

All bridges will now be ashes, friends and relatives just a distant memory. You've cut all ties with clubs, hobbies, and church, no longer file tax returns, and will never again work for an employer. You may feel this is necessary if there's a bounty on your head or a contract on your life, but at this point, is life still worth living?

If so, keep running, because you can *still* be found. The PI, however, must now have *unlimited* funds at his disposal, and will call for help. Just as pinned-down soldiers on a battlefield can call in air strikes, PIs can call in investigative reporters. These are the men who dig up celebrity skeletons for tabloids such as the *National Enquirer*, *Globe*, and—until Rupert Murdoch had to shut it down—the tabloid newspaper *The Sun*. Never underestimate an investigative reporter. These guys may sometimes go to jail—as in the Murdoch scandal—but until they do, they are the best in the business.

I recommend you start working on Level One even before you finish reading this book. In the weeks and months to come, raise yourself to Level Two—the choice of the majority of my readers.

After that, decide whether or not you wish to ease up to Level Three. It may look difficult at first, but countless others have done it and so can you. Not only may it be easier than you think, but it can be fun as well, and lead you to a more stress-free life.

Now let's talk about four more levels:

THE FOUR LEVELS OF PURSUIT

The first three levels will normally be a private investigator hired by a law firm, a disgruntled stockholder, an ex-lover, an ex-employee, a stalker, a creditor, or any weirdo out for what he or she considers revenge.

LEVEL ONE

The average small-city one-person PI. He (they are still usually male, though that is slowly changing) sits at his desk and runs whatever data he's been given, using paid national and international databases, common Internet searches, and social media site searches. He may make phone calls to family and friends or church members if the client has provided that contact information. A PI in Tennessee once outlined his standard method of searching for assets:

> The first thing I do when I search for hidden assets is pull the subject's credit report. I look for credit cards, ATMs, etc., issued by banks. Some small banks like the ones you describe automatically issue these cards. You'd have to specifically tell them you don't want them, otherwise they appear on your credit report and the bank is exposed.

If he doesn't find you with that method, or in the phone book, he'll usually give up. This type of PI is not normally ready to break any laws, and often makes less than $50,000 a year.

LEVEL TWO

Sometimes works in gray areas. Is less risk-averse. Is more tenacious and better at networking with subcontractors and contacts inside anything from DMVs and cable companies to cell phone providers and sometimes even police departments. If you have property, vehicles, phones, cable TV, electricity, disposal service, professional or business licenses, or anything else in your name, run for cover!

They'll find your employer, family and friends, religious and political affiliations, former school mates and professors. They'll find and search through your financial records in any country. If the legal circumstances exist, they can obtain your school transcripts, or conduct surveillance using sophisticated equipment. They earn mid-to-high-five-figure incomes along the coasts.

LEVEL THREE

Will subcontract the *legal* portions of an investigation to the Level Two PIs or to info-brokers. Will bend or break any law if the price is right (think Anthony Pellicano and Chris Butler). They will run credit reports, grab school transcripts and medical information, or search financial records without permission or permissible purpose.

They'll bribe police, plant evidence, hire crooks for surreptitious entries and muggers who will take you down to check your wallet for ID, run brothels for information on their clients, and even hire lowlifes who will hold your feet to the fire to get the information they've been paid to collect. (Former government agents-turned-corporate espionage agents run in these circles.) Makes a high six-to-seven-figure income until caught.

LEVEL FOUR

Government agents from whatever nation. Sovereignty means nothing to these people (think Osama bin Laden). At this level, give up, jump off a high bridge, or go the route outlined in chapter 24. No life insurance company will insure you.

Sometimes, however, your worst enemy will turn out to be . . . YOU. That's why the next subtitle is:

"WHOM SHALL I CONFIDE IN?"

A short, balding man named Stanley Mark Rifkin worked at the Security Pacific National Bank in Los Angeles. Security Pacific thought of him as a computer programmer, but Rifkin thought of himself as a consummate thief.

On October 25, he entered the bank, crossed the lobby, and took the elevator up to the wire transfer room. From this room, hundreds of millions of dollars passed every day from Security Pacific through the Federal Reserve system and on to international banks. Rifkin, who identified himself as the bank's computer consultant, was not challenged as he walked into the heavily guarded room. By interviewing one of the workers, he learned the routing instructions, transfer routines, and the day's security code. Before he left, he memorized an employee access code from an information board on the wall. Later that day, posing as a branch manager, he called the wire room.

"This is Mike Hansen on International."

"Okay, and the office number?" a friendly female voice asked.

"It's 286."

"And the code?"

"Code is 4739."

"Okay."

Now came the moment Rifkin had been living for.

"The bank," he said, speaking in a calm voice, "is Irving Trust in New York City. Payment is to Wozchod Bank, Zurich, Switzerland. The amount is ten million two hundred thousand even."

"Okay, and what's the interoffice settlement number?"

"Let me check. I'll call you right back." He then phoned a different number at the bank. Pretending to be someone working in the wire room, he asked for the settlement number. They gave it to him, and he called the wire room back. The clerk typed his order into the system. Rifkin had just pulled off one of the largest bank thefts in history. Before the day was out, he was high above the Atlantic, bound for Europe.

In Switzerland, he purchased 250,000 raw diamonds, weighing nearly four pounds. (Raw diamonds are easy to sell and cannot be traced.) At this point, it appeared that Rifkin had pulled off the perfect crime. *No one at Security Pacific even knew the money was gone!* Then he returned to the United States.

Some say he had an ego problem, and couldn't help showing the diamonds to his friends. Others say Rifkin tried to work with a friend to sell the diamonds. Whatever the case, *someone* told the FBI. They chased him, caught him, and he went to prison.

Francis Beaumont, one of England's most popular playwrights in the Age of Shakespeare, had this to say about secrets:

> All confidence which is not absolute and entire is dangerous. There are few occasions but where a man ought either to say all, or conceal all, for, how little ever you have revealed of your secret to a friend, you have already said too much if you think it not safe to make him privy to all particulars.

Allow me to rephrase his comment, boiled down to plain language of the present day:

> *Do not reveal confidential information—and especially not your home address—to your attorney, CPA, banker, doctor, dentist, school authorities, relatives, family, friends, or anyone else unless you would trust them with your life.*

WHAT THIS BOOK IS ABOUT

This book is about how to keep your private life *private*. It is not about avoiding taxes or about protecting your assets from creditors, although the latter may be an added benefit. Nor is it a call to disobey the law. I consider myself a law-abiding, tax-paying citizen of the world. True, I may not be accurate when called upon to give my home address, and I do confess that I am allergic to certain kinds of permits. You, then, make your own decision. (Although I've made privacy my business for more than fifty years, I am not a lawyer. So never take any questionable measure without the advice and counsel of a trained legal professional.)

For example, you may wish to operate a legitimate but anonymous business from your home. This means you may have to ignore the requirements for a business license and also the resale tax permit (assuming you live in a sales-tax state). The city will lose a small fee when you don't pay for a license. On the other hand, the state will gain when you pay sales taxes for supplies that might otherwise be exempt. Other small pluses and minuses will enter in. Depending upon the community, there may or may not be any penalty if you are caught, other than catching up on some payment you failed to make. So then, please note:

> *If I mention any procedure, which I suspect might be construed as illegal in some states or provinces, I will warn you of that fact beforehand. My responsibility is to explain the options. Your responsibility is to make your own decisions.*

WHAT MAKES THIS BOOK UNIQUE?

AUTHOR'S QUALIFICATIONS

Malcolm Gladwell, in his best-selling book *Outliers: The Story of Success*, repeatedly mentions the "10,000-Hour Rule," stating that the key to success in any field is, to a large extent, a matter of practicing a specific task for a total of around 10,000 hours.

Since 1959, my studies in the field of privacy have surpassed that figure by far.

ALTERNATIVE TO DELAWARE AND NEVADA CORPORATIONS

I recommend a legal entity that, formed correctly, can almost certainly never be traced back to you.

NO RANTING OR RAVING

Well, a little ranting maybe, but unlike many other authors, no raving about government corruption, black helicopters, jack-booted thugs, or the Internal Revenue Service. This book is about Life in the Real World, not a treatise about the Constitution, the Bill of Rights, or Common Law.

UP-TO-DATE ADVICE FOR THE PRESENT TIME

Although no book can be completely up to the minute, since laws and procedures are constantly changing, I maintain both a Web site (www.howtobeinvisible.com) and a blog (blog.invisible-privacy.com), to keep readers up to date. Go there for the latest information about personal and business privacy. Be sure to sign up for the news via e-mails, as well.

INTERNATIONAL SLANT

Most books on privacy—including the previous editions of this book—have been written specifically for Americans. The reason is that Americans are under more attacks for frivolous lawsuits, tracked by more PIs, targeted for more asset seizures by the Treasury Department, and jailed for more "Homeland Security" charges than any place else on the planet.

Compare the United States to other nations (figures are approximate):

United States	737 in jail, per 100,000 people
South Africa	402 in jail, per 100,000 people
Thailand	340 in jail, per 100,000 people
Chile	204 in jail, per 100,000 people
Israel	174 in jail, per 100,000 people
Mexico	169 in jail, per 100,000 people
New Zealand	160 in jail, per 100,000 people
England, Wales	152 in jail, per 100,000 people
Spain	144 in jail, per 100,000 people
China	119 in jail, per 100,000 people
Canada	116 in jail, per 100,000 people
Australia	116 in jail, per 100,000 people
Netherlands	112 in jail, per 100,000 people
Germany	96 in jail, per 100,000 people
Andorra	90 in jail, per 100,000 people
Sweden	75 in jail, per 100,000 people
Norway	64 in jail, per 100,000 people
Iceland	40 in jail, per 100,000 people
Nigeria	33 in jail, per 100,000 people

Nevertheless, the entire world is now changing, and not for the better. I am currently getting visitors to my Web site from more than seventy countries and territories—something I would not have imagined even two or three years ago. For that reason I have included chapter 27: "International Privacy 101."

HOW TO USE THIS BOOK

Each chapter provides you with basic, step-by-step information. Although I suggest you read the chapters in order, you may decide to skip some that you feel do not apply to you. However—

Do not skip the next chapter.

Your journey to invisibility must begin with the first step: *separating your name from your home address.*

SEPARATE YOUR NAME FROM YOUR HOME ADDRESS

Consider the case of George Joseph Cvek, as presented in the book *Diary of a D.A.* by Martin M. Frank, formerly an assistant district attorney in the Bronx. Frank writes:

When the doorbell rang on that January afternoon, a young housewife opened her apartment door to find a slim, ordinary-looking man of about twenty-eight standing at the threshold. He was a stranger to her.

"Are you Mrs. Allen?" he asked.

"Yes, I am."

"Is your husband home?"

"No," she replied, "he isn't here now."

"Gee, I'm sorry," he said. "I know him from Norwalk, Connecticut. I thought this was his early day. Maybe I'll come back tonight." He seemed rather well acquainted with her husband, a route salesman in Connecticut for a bakery company.

The caller half-turned to go, then stopped and apologetically asked, "Could I have a drink of water?"

Sure," she said, "wait here a second." Leaving him at the door, Mrs. Allen went into the kitchen. When she returned, she found that he had walked through the foyer into the living room and was seated on the sofa. . . .

The caller continued to deceive Mrs. Allen and then suddenly struck her down and prepared to rape her. At that moment, the telephone rang. He jumped up and ran from the apartment, slamming the door behind him. But in the years to come, more than 200 women were not so fortunate. Their telephones did not ring. In each case, the caller gained entrance by telling the wife he knew her husband, and after gaining entrance through subterfuge, he raped and killed her, then burglarized the home.

In each case it was the husbands themselves who had unwittingly made the crime possible. They had picked up a neatly dressed hitchhiker—George Joseph Cvek—who said he was from Boys Town, Nebraska, and given him a ride. When Cvek was dropped off, he asked the drivers for their *home address* so he could show his appreciation for the ride by mailing him a small gift. At that instant, *each husband sealed his wife's death warrant.*

> Note: More than half the people who come to me for help are
> at the time receiving both mail and packages at their home
> address. In my opinion, this is an incredible error, a matter of
> life and death.

An extreme viewpoint? Mike Ketcher of Burnsville, Minnesota, editor of *The Financial Privacy Report*, certainly doesn't think so. He hired Yon Son Moon, a divorced woman, to work in his office. Yon Son's ex-husband, Jae Choe, had been harassing her for years. When Mike hired Yon Son, Choe was furious. Eventually he went on a rampage, shooting Yon Son, their fourteen-year-old son John, and two policemen, after which he killed himself. The publisher of the newsletter, Daniel Rosenthal, sums up the two important lessons learned, as follows:

> *First,* if you think the police are there to protect you, let me tell you differently. Yon Son had a restraining order against Choe. So did we, at our home and our office. But the police ignored our repeated requests to enforce these restraining orders, despite Choe's continual violations and threats. On several occasions they literally laughed at our requests for enforcement.

> *Second,* when the police don't work, privacy DOES work. The only person in our company that was truly safe was Mike Ketcher. He was safe because he kept his personal affairs so private that Mr. Choe couldn't find him.

Hiding your home address is not easy, but it's doable, one step at a time. The first step is to immediately stop sending and receiving mail at your home address.

MAIL THEFT

A Seattle newspaper runs a "Rant & Rave" section each Sunday. Readers can call in during the week with whatever they wish to praise or condemn. Here's one of them:

> *A big rant to the felon who stole our outgoing U.S. mail, forcing several people to close bank accounts and depriving friends and relatives of holiday greetings and children and grandchildren of their Christmas checks.*

Does anything about this rant sound a little strange to you? What if the reader's message had started out like this?

> *A big rant to the person who saw us park our car on the street, loaded with Christmas packages, and walk away. Although we did*

leave the doors open and the key in the ignition, he had no right to get in and drive away. . . .

When you walk out to the curb, place your mail in the box, and raise the red flag, your mail is as vulnerable to theft as your car would be if you left the key in it and the doors open.

Every day more than 100,000 residential mailboxes in the United States are burglarized. This applies to mail being received both in the city and in the country, both in private homes and in apartment complexes. In Hammond, Indiana, before they were finally arrested, two men and a woman went from door to door but did not knock or ring any bells. The neighbors saw nothing more suspicious than each person depositing an advertising brochure in each mailbox. What they didn't see was the sleight of hand when the person traded the brochure for whatever mail was in the box.

More than a year prior to the rant about theft from a mailbox, the same Seattle newspaper had run a series of articles warning of mail theft not only from home mailboxes but from mail collection boxes on the street, plus the boxes used at thousands of apartments, condominiums, and commercial buildings in the Pacific Northwest. For months, thieves had been using counterfeit "arrow keys." Each arrow key provides access to about 2,500 mail collection boxes, more than 10,000 apartments and condominiums, and virtually all office and commercial buildings in the region. (The keys give postal workers easy access to the mailboxes, making it easier for them to pick up and deliver messages and packages.)

Readers were urged to stop using outside mailboxes to deposit mail, including their own home mailboxes. Instead, they were to deposit mail only inside a post office. In addition to professional thieves, it was said that many others have been stealing mail: drug addicts, to support their habit; teenagers, looking for cash; petty thieves, looking for any number of things.

In the article, headlined "Theft of Mail a Problem at Our Doorstep," U.S. Postal Inspector Jim Bordenet voiced mail security concerns.

> "Thieves rifle outgoing mail for checks written to pay bills. They then alter the checks so they can cash them for large amounts." He suggests people not put outgoing mail into their own boxes, and especially advises against using the red flag, which is a signal to thieves. "Thieves sometimes follow carriers around and steal incoming mail," he said. "They're typically looking for boxes of checks and credit-card offers."

I will spare you the flurry of follow-up articles and letters to the editor that followed publication of the article just quoted. Some of the questions raised were:

- Why didn't the Postal Service warn the public about such thefts years ago?
- Why was nothing said until the thefts were exposed by the local newspapers?
- Why—even now—is the problem not being solved?

Another article, this one from the McClatchy Newspapers, is datelined Sacramento, California, and titled "Post Office Fights Mailbox Theft." It reports that hundreds of pieces of mail are stolen daily in the Sacramento area. In rural areas the criminals watch for raised red flags, the signal that outgoing mail is inside. Others pry open "cluster boxes" at apartment complexes or housing developments and steal everybody's mail at the same time. In some cases they even pry open the standard blue U.S. mail collection boxes. The article quotes Tom Hall, a postal inspector who investigates mail theft from Sacramento to the Oregon border:

> Today, thanks to chemicals and computers, thieves can use almost any kind of financial information to commit a variety of

financial crimes. If you write a check to a utility and a bad guy gets it, he can "wash" the utility's name off and make the check out to himself in a higher amount. With that one check, he can also make himself a whole new set of checks under your name.

Even worse, continues the article, "some criminals 'assume' the victim's identity and apply for credit cards in the victim's name."

In an upscale neighborhood in Campbell, California, mail was being stolen on a regular basis. The thief was an elegant-appearing woman who dressed in expensive clothing so that she would not attract attention when she walked up to houses and stole the mail. Remember, all these thieves need is your name, address, account number, and credit information. They then get on the phone and order merchandise through catalogues.

If your home is vacant during the day, they may even have the products sent to your home. They'll just park along your street and wait for FedEx or UPS to swing by. My advice, therefore, is to deposit all outgoing mail inside a local post office. You will thus protect your outgoing mail not only from random theft but from having it surreptitiously read. (Some Level Three PIs may "borrow" the mail from your home mailbox, read it, and return it the next day, apparently unopened.)

However, if dropping your mail off at a post office is not practical, perhaps you could drop it off at work. (Check first, of course, to see where *that* mail is dropped off.) Or, you might drop it in one of those big blue mailboxes at shopping centers and other public places. Even there, however, it is best to do it just before the listed pickup time.

If you are still in doubt about the dangers of mail theft, google "mail theft." (Enclose the two words with quotation marks, as shown.) You'll get about a quarter of a million sites to check out.

MAIL-FORWARDING APPLICATION

Do not check the little circle marked "Permanent." If you do, your name will go into the Postal Service's National Change of Address list and this list of persons who have moved is sold to the commercial mail-list folks and thus your name and new address will go into countless computers.

Instead, check the "Temporary" box and give a date when this is to end. At that point, notify the post office that you are closing the P.O. box and do not wish to have any mail forwarded. Mail will then be returned to sender.

TAKE THIS IMMEDIATE STEP TO PROTECT YOUR MAIL

If you are presently receiving mail at home, turn in a forwarding address. But where should this mail go? Certainly not to any permanent address you will use in the future. The following are some options:

1. If you presently have a PO box, choose that address.
2. Have it sent on to your place of business if you have one, or perhaps to a friend who is in business.
3. Rent a box at a commercial mail-receiving agency (CMRA).
4. Obtain a ghost address (of which more will be said later) in some faraway state or country and have the mail sent there.

ADDITIONAL FAMILY BENEFIT

When mail is received at home, a curious child may open a letter that has a bank statement, a notice from a creditor, bad news from a law firm, or whatever. Having your mail delivered elsewhere avoids this possibility.

Because the secure sending and receiving of mail has become so complicated, the question-and-answer section that follows is one of the largest in this book. If you are in a hurry, however, jump to the next chapter. You can always come back.

QUESTIONS & ANSWERS

What is a "mail cover"?

This is a system used by a number of governments to check your mail without a court order. Your mailman, or the clerk that "boxes" your mail will be instructed to note the return addresses and country of origin of your incoming mail. If you live a squeaky-clean life, you may say to yourself, imitating *Mad* magazine's Alfred E. Neuman, "What? Me worry?" Read on:

Suppose you send mail *to* a person or company that is the subject of a mail cover? If you list your name and return address, you yourself could end up on a suspect list. There are at least two obvious solutions:

1. Copy the British—eliminate a return address.
2. Use some other return address, far, far away.

Recently, the postal authorities are getting more cautious, e.g., the current requirement of making you take any parcel weighing more than thirteen ounces to the counter, in person. For such parcels, they will insist you include a return address. The day may soon be here when a return address will be required on all letters as well.

I send out large volumes of mail, so I use a postage meter. Any danger there?

I don't know how large a volume you refer to, but with one of my previous businesses, my wife and I used to mail 2,000 letters a week. We had a regular system, using self-adhesive stamps. First,

we stuck one stamp on each of four fingers, then we put them on
4 envelopes, one, two, three, four, and repeat.

Why didn't we use a postage meter? Because each postage
meter has an identification number that ties it to a renter and to
a specific location, that's why.

*Does it matter if—unsure of the exact postage—I put on
more than enough stamps?*

Judge for yourself. I know of a case in Missouri where a man put
$38 postage on a small package that weighed less than two
pounds. Destination, Los Angeles, but it didn't arrive. In view of
the excess postage, the DEA (Drug Enforcement Administration) was called in, and the package turned out to contain $10,000
in cash. Although I do not know if the source of the money was
legal, I do know that the DEA "arrests" and keeps most confiscated cash, even though the owner may never be convicted of
anything.

Actually, cash can be mailed most anywhere using many envelopes and small sums per envelope. With $38, the Missourian
could have bought eighty-six first-class stamps. Had he then put
just four $100 bills in each envelope, wrapping the money with
a page or two from a magazine, he could have mailed out, not
$10,000, but $34,400. And if mailed on different days from
various post offices, and with a variety of fictitious return addresses, would anyone even have a clue?

This was not the first time I heard of incorrect postage alert-
ing the authorities. One of the telltale signs postal inspectors
look for, in the case of letter bombs, is excess postage. I use an
unusually accurate electronic scale and double-check all outgoing mail.

*At present, I receive a daily newspaper in my own name. It
goes into its own box alongside my rural mailbox. Is there*

some way to at least continue to receive my daily paper, both at my present home, and at the new one when I move?

At one time we had a Canadian newspaper delivered directly to a holiday home under another name. No longer. Too many cases like the one cited in Carson City's *Nevada Appeal,* headed, "Minden Teen Appears in Court, May Face 15 Charges." The charges were that three teenagers burglarized houses in the Carson Valley *while the occupants were away.* And how did they know the occupants were away? From "information allegedly obtained through his job as a newspaper carrier." Nevertheless, if you cannot live without your daily newspaper(s), then at least heed this advice:

- Cancel the newspaper you now receive. A month later, order a new subscription under another name. Avoid paying the newspaper carrier in person.

- When you leave on a trip, do not have the newspapers held. Get a friend or neighbor to pick them up. (Nevertheless, the best way is still to have the newspaper delivered to your ghost address.)

How secure is my incoming mail?

That depends on where it's coming from, what it looks like, and who your enemies are. Under normal circumstances, I have far more confidence in regular mail (often referred to as snail mail) than in most electronic mail, because there is no possible way to scan the interiors of *all* letters in the U.S. postal system at any one time. Contrast this with electronic mail, which can be computer-searched at every junction along the way, red-flagging messages with any of hundreds or thousands of key words such as *bomb, gas, gun, rifle, money, cash,* or with any specific name including yours.

Note, however, that certain government officials *do* monitor mail from tax-haven countries, especially those on the following list:

Antigua	Germany	Netherlands
Aruba	Great Britain	Nigeria
Austria	Guernsey	Pakistan
Bahamas	Hong Kong	Panama
Belize	Hungary	Russia
Bermuda	Iran	Saudi Arabia
British Virgin Islands	Isle of Man	Singapore
Cayman Islands	Latvia	Switzerland
Channel Islands	Liberia	Thailand
Columbia	Liechtenstein	Turks and Caicos Islands
Cook Islands	Lithuania	United Arab Emirates
Ecuador	Luxembourg	Uruguay
Estonia	Marshall Islands	Vanuatu
Gibraltar	Nauru	Venezuela
	Nevis	

Also, what do your incoming letters look like? If you are in my age bracket, you may remember when your mother dripped hot red wax on the flap of an envelope, then pressed a seal into the wax before it cooled. The more modern method is to seal the flaps with clear tape. Neither is secure, and both methods (especially the red wax seal!) draw unwanted attention to the envelope, saying: "Something valuable in here."

Further, anyone with a spray can of freon gas—sold under various trade names in spy shops—can read what's inside without opening the envelope at all. When hit with the spray, the envelope becomes transparent. Thirty seconds later, as the gas evaporates, it returns to its normal condition, with no evidence of this intrusion. (To find out if this is happening, have your sender mail you an innocuous letter, using a felt-tip pen for addressing the envelope. The ink will run when carbon tetrachloride is used—thus tipping you off that the mail was read.)

Methods once confined to the CIA are now common knowledge, thanks to Amazon.com. They offer used copies of the *CIA Flaps and Seals Manual* that carefully details "surreptitious entries of highly protected items of mail," and removing and replacing seals and using carbon tetrachloride on tape. What worries the CIA and other surreptitious readers of secret mail is not the sealed or taped envelope, but the normal one. "The most innocuous-looking envelope," says the CIA manual, "may be the one that will get the operator in the most trouble." Correct! See the following question and answer about innocuous-looking envelopes.

How I can best protect my outgoing mail?

First of all, *the envelope should appear normal.* A junk-mail appearance is best (as long as the recipient knows that in advance), and for that reason I prefer a standard #10 envelope with a laser-printed label. If a sealed, taped, or otherwise obviously protected envelope is desired, enclose and protect everything in a #9 envelope and insert that one in the #10 envelope. If you are not familiar with U.S. envelope numbers, note these measurements:

#10 envelope: $4 \frac{1}{8} \times 9 \frac{1}{2}$ in. (10.5 × 24 cm.)
#9 envelope: $3 \frac{7}{8} \times 8 \frac{7}{8}$ in. (10 × 22.5 cm.)

To counteract the envelope's transparency when sprayed with freon, wrap the contents of the #9 envelope with carbon paper, if you can still find it in this modern age.

What's the best way to have a letter remailed from some faraway place?

For a few years after the anthrax scare that followed the events of 9/11, it was best not to even think about remailing a letter.

However, the scare seems to have receded, so I'll suggest a method that usually works quite well.

Prepare your letter, seal it in an addressed #9 envelope (available at any office-supply store), and put on the correct postage. Enclose your letter in a #10 envelope, add a cover letter as shown below, and a $5 bill. Note that you don't use a last name, so there is no way to prove you were not a guest.

> *Sheraton El Conquistador*
> *Attention: Concierge*
> *I was a recent guest at your hotel, and most impressed with your fine service. I do, however, have a small problem, and I must ask you a favor.*
> *During my Arizona stay, I promised to write to a friend about an errand he gave me, and also to an associate while in Tucson. I forgot to do both things, so would you kindly help me cover my derrière by mailing the enclosed items?*
> *I enclose $5 for your trouble, and hope to thank you in person when I return to the Sheraton El Conquistador later this year.*
> *Yours sincerely,*
> *Jim*

Mail your letter to "Concierge" at one of the very best hotels in the city of your choice. (You can get the name and address from AAA, or off the Internet.) Here is a sample of how to address the envelope:

For the CONCIERGE:
Sheraton El Conquistador
10000 North Oracle Road
Tucson, Arizona 85737

Note: If there is some doubt that the hotel has a concierge, just address the letter to "Reception." (If there isn't a reception desk, you've chosen too small a hotel.)

From now on, when you travel, pick up sample envelopes and letterheads from luxury hotels. Staying at them is best, but you can often just drift up to the desk when they're busy with check-ins and kindly ask for "a sheet of paper and an envelope." One of each is enough, as you'll never use a specific hotel for remailing more than once.

Does the U.S. Postal Service take a picture of every letter I send out, and if so, should I be worried?

When I first discovered this information some years ago. I wondered what the purpose of this was, how long the pictures were kept on file, and whether or not the back of the envelope was also being photographed. Thanks to a friend inside the USPS, I now have the facts. The following is what happens when you mail a letter:

1. The front side of your envelope is photographed. At the same time, a fine color barcode is sprayed on the back side of your letter.

2. The image is then sent to a remote site, usually in another state where non-postal workers work at terminals and key in the barcode for that specific letter.

3. Your letter then is processed through a machine that reads the light-colored barcode on the back side and instantly sprays a regular barcode on the lower front side of the envelope. (However, if a letter already has a barcode on it, it will usually not have its picture taken. For example, mail from utility companies gets bypassed from this process.)

"I don't know how long those images are stored for," says my informant. "However, my guess is that it no longer than a few days."

* * *

Conclusion: Normally, it makes no difference whether you put a return address on the front or the back of the envelope. However, mail handlers can make a note of the return addresses you are using, if they have a legitimate reason for doing so. If, therefore, you are concerned about certain sensitive mail, one suggestion would be to not include a return address on your outgoing mail.

A better solution, however, would be to use a ghost address for the return. That way, you will know if your letter failed to arrive. (It may be returned for insufficient postage or for an error in the address. These things happen to the best of us.) It will also prevent your letter from ending up in Atlanta, Saint Paul, or San Francisco. These are the USPS's three major mail recovery centers and once your letter gets there, it *will* be opened and examined.

WHEN IS A "LIE" NOT A LIE?

In your quest for personal privacy, again and again you will come up against questions like these:

- What is your name?
- What is your home telephone number?
- What is your street address?
- What is your date of birth?
- What is your Social Security number?

Also, if you are (for example) a husband and father who is determined to keep the family's private affairs private, be prepared for questions like these:

Wife: What? You want me to *lie*?

Child: Daddy, did you just tell a *lie*?

Parents: What do you mean, we can't tell anyone where you really live? You want us to *lie*, son?

Since lying is a moral issue, and since morality is basically a religious issue, I am going to cite the exact words from a small religious magazine I read back in 1954. It was published by the

International Bible Students Association, and since it answered a question I had long wondered about, I memorized this sentence word for word:

> A LIE is a false statement made by one to another, who is entitled to hear and know the truth, and which false statement tends toward injury to the other.

This is the only definition of a lie I've ever read that covers untrue statements made by the biblical characters Abraham, Sarah, Isaac, David, Jonathan, and Rahab. Did they disgrace themselves as liars by their caution? Not according to the above definition.

You, dear reader, must make your own evaluation . . . and accept the responsibility. What I have to say here is about decisions I myself have made. Although they are presented merely as guidelines for your meditation, I recommend them. For example:

1. Where no harm will be done, and no sworn oath is involved, I often give incorrect information. So does my wife.
2. I never give incorrect information if I am to sign a sworn statement, whether or not before a notary.
3. I may *withhold* information from the police or from government representative but I won't lie to them.
4. Under no condition whatsoever will I file a false tax return.

Here is an example of 1, above. When I open a new e-mail account, I know that the instructions call for me to enter my true name, address, etc. However, since I do not plan to defraud anyone, I list anything *but* the true facts. At other times, I am asked my date of birth. Although it is listed correctly on my driver's license and on my passport, elsewhere the date ranges from January 1, 1926, to December 31, 1935.

Here is an example of 2: I was recently in Vancouver, British Columbia, planning to buy a cell phone scanner and bring it into the United States. (They are legal in Canada, but illegal in the

United States) Since I was not prepared to hide this purchase from the U.S. customs office, I planned to ship it over the border via UPS. The manager of the electronics store brought out a form and suggested "we" could list the scanner as something else. However, when I read the customs form, I saw that I would have to sign a sworn statement that the above description was true. No sale.

Example of 3: As I was reviewing this chapter, I was stopped by a cop in State A. My SUV has State A license plates, but my driver's license is from State B. The registration shows a New Mexico LLC with an address in Spain. The license plate holder reads "Arrecife de Lanzarote" on top, and "Canary Islands, Spain" on the bottom. The cop said he'd stopped me because I made a left turn into a far lane, and for not wearing a seatbelt. He took my license, walked back to his patrol car, and checked both the DL and the plates. (My last ticket had been about twelve years ago, for speeding.) When he returned, he made no mention of the LLC, nor its foreign address.

Cop: Do you live here in [State A] now? (Referring to the DL from State B.)

Me: "I travel back and forth." (Correct, but I withheld the additional information that I only return to State B when it's time to renew my driver's license in person, which is once every eight years.)

I also confess to withholding information in other ways. If I run a small business out of my home, I neglect to get a business license. If I move, I neglect to inform the postal authorities. If asked for information when obtaining an e-mail address, I fail to list my true name and home address. You, the reader, have three choices:

1. You can follow the pattern I have set.
2. You can tell no untruth under any circumstance.
3. You can lie about everything and sign anything, true or not.

In the chapters to come, I will assume you have chosen option 1. From time to time I may add a suggestion for those of you who stick with option 2. As for any who go for option 3, I'd truly appreciate it if you'd take this book back to the store and demand a refund of your money. This is not your kind of book.

PIS AND TRUE LIES

Now we come to the gray area—the hiring of a private investigator (PI). The shades of gray vary from light to just a millimeter above inky black. The PIs call it "pretexting" but you and I know what it really is, and if you hire him, are you not responsible for what he does?

EXAMPLE OF HOW PRETEXTING WORKS

For a brief time, Karl and Lorelei are lovers. When Karl turns violent, Lorelei walks out. Karl stalks her. She read this same book you are reading and follows the advice by moving away and changing everything. She also picks up a double barrel shotgun. When Karl discovers Lorelei has dropped out of sight, he vows that if he cannot have her, then no one else will have her, either. He buys a used handgun, makes his plans, and then goes to Guido. Guido has a reputation for tracking down anyone, anywhere, anytime.

Karl gives Guido a made-up sob story and the PI accepts it. He takes a hefty retainer from Karl and writes down the four pieces of information that Karl gives him: her full name, Social Security number, former address, and the name of a hospital where she was once briefly admitted.

The PI promises Karl results within twenty-four hours. Actually, Guido will have Lorelei's new address in less than sixty minutes, obtained with just two short "pretext" telephone calls. The first is to Plano General Hospital.

PGH: Hello, please hold. *Long pause.*

PGH: Plano General Hospital, may I help you?

Guido: Yes, this is John, with Dr. Childress's office in Mc-Kinney, and I'm processing some insurance forms for Lorelei Altbusser. Could you pull that file for me? I need the date of admission.

PGH: Do you have her Social Security number?

Guido: Let's see [*makes sound of papers shuffling*]. Yeah, it's 987-65-4325.

PGH: Okay, please hold for a minute while I get the file. [*Pause.*]

PGH: Okay, got it. She was admitted 10-10-2011.

Guido: What was the complaint?

PGH: Looks like persistent pains following a recent abortion.

Guido: Does it indicate any treatment?

PGH: Looks like there was a prescription, was all.

Guido: Well, thanks for the help, and—oh, one more thing. On the form she filled out, does it list her mother's name as Mary Altbusser, with telephone 344-1288?

PGH: No, her admittance form lists next-of-kin as Gertrude Altbusser at 478-1991.

Guido: Muchas gracias, and have a nice day.

Next, the PI calls 478-1991 because he figures Lorelei keeps in contact with her mother. Once again, he represents himself as a doctor.

Guido: Gertrude Altbusser, please.

Mother: Yes, this is she.

Guido: Mrs. Altbusser, this is Dr. Noe at the Cook County Morgue. We have a body here that's been tentatively identified as a Lorelei Altbusser. Do you have a daughter by that name?

Mother: Oh, my God! Oh no! Oh God!

Guido: Mrs. Altbusser, is your daughter an African-American?

Mother: No, no, my daughter is white!
[*Guido's reason for whipsawing this poor woman back and forth is to inject her with truth serum. Now she will tell him what he wants to know.*]

Guido: Mrs. Altbusser, how do you explain this dead black girl having your daughter's driver's license?

Mother: I don't know. Maybe Lorelei's purse was stolen?

Guido: Mrs. Altbusser, when's the last time you spoke with your daughter?

Mother: I talked to her last Sunday. She's a good girl, she calls me every Sunday.

Guido: Mrs. Altbusser, it's very important we speak with your daughter on this matter without delay. How can I get in touch with her immediately?

Mother: She's living in Odessa now, and doesn't have a phone in her apartment. She works at a Circle K on Central Drive. I could give you that number. . . .

Guido: Yes, please give it to me now, ma'am.

Mother: It's 960-362-0464.

Guido: Thank you, Mrs. Altbusser.

Author's Note: When hearing the lie about a dead body, mothers often get hysterical. One PI, writing about this routine, says, "I've heard of cases where the mother has literally dropped the phone in midsentence and raced over to the County Morgue!"

PRIVATE INVESTIGATORS—FRIENDS OR FOES?

In the foregoing example, *from Lorelei's viewpoint*, the PI was just a miserable liar-for-hire who should have checked Karl's story out before taking the job. When Karl breaks into her home with a gun, we all hope she lets him have it with both barrels to the belly. But now, let's change the context. Suppose the one who goes to the PI is *you*, and this time the PI is Paulo, Guido's brother. Paulo is just like Guido except that before he takes the case, he verifies your story.

Your rebellious fourteen-year-old daughter has just run away from home with some guy from Chicago named Armen Bedrosian who is in his thirties. You call the Cook County Police, but all you get is a runaround. You go to Paulo. After checking you out, he takes the case. A quick check with his database accounts on the Internet show that Armen is an ex-con who was jailed in his teens for rape and attempted murder. He's been back on the streets for only two months. The PI tracks Armen down by first locating his mother. He calls her.

"Mrs. Bedrosian, this is Dr. Noe at the Cook County Morgue. We have a body here that's been tentatively identified as Armen Bedrosian. Do you have a son by that name . . . ?"

Even if the PI had to resort to pretexts in order to save your underage daughter, will you nevertheless not thank him to the end of your days?

MAILBOXES, PUBLIC
AND PRIVATE

By "public," I mean the boxes you can rent at a government postal service such as the United States Postal Service (USPS).

By "private," I refer to commercial mail-receiving agencies (CMRAs) such as Parcel Plus, Packaging Store, Pak Mail Centers of America, Postal Annex, PostNet Postal and Business Centers, and The UPS Store. This chapter will show you a fast and simple way to achieve a basic level of privacy and security.

If you do not already have a post-office box, you may wish to obtain one for your personal mail. Then, you could rent a private mailbox from a CMRA and use both your name and a made-up "company name" for business mail, magazine subscriptions, and deliveries from FedEx and UPS.

Until such time as you move, of course, your present street address will be in dozens—or more likely, hundreds—of databases. However, from this moment on, you will never again give out your street address. Then, when you move, and follow the advice in the chapters to come, you will drop below the radar.

However, before you make any changes, make sure you both read *and understand* this chapter and the one that follows.

POST-OFFICE BOXES

If a choice is available, rent a box as far away from your home as is convenient for picking up mail once or twice a week. The ideal situation—often the case if you have a long commute to work—is to have the box in another town. This is sometimes possible for those who live in "twin" cities. (If you live in East Minneapolis, get a box in West St. Paul.)

ADVANTAGES

First and foremost, you avoid having to give out your street address. In addition:

- If you move to another location in the same area, there will be no changes to make for incoming mail.
- Your mail will be safe from thieves, no matter how long you leave it in the box.
- When you are on vacation, mail will not pile up at the mailbox at your home—a clear signal that the occupants are away.

DISADVANTAGES

The biggest single disadvantage of getting a post-office box is the process you have to go through. Prior to the passage of the U.S. Patriot Act (officially "Uniting and Strengthening America by Providing Appropriate Tools Required to Intercept and Obstruct Terrorism Act of 2001"), it was fairly easy to rent a PO box and retain your privacy. This is no longer the case. Thus:

- You must show two forms of ID, and one of them must show your current home address. (This violates the rule of never allowing your true name to be coupled with your true home address.)
- If you list other persons who will also be receiving mail at this address, they, too, must now furnish two forms of identification.
- If in the United States, you must sign PS Form 1093 right next to this chilling statement:

  Signature of Applicant: *I certify that all information furnished on this form is accurate, truthful, and complete. I understand that anyone who furnishes false or misleading information on this form or omits information requested on this form may be subject to criminal and/or civil penalties, including fines and imprisonment.*

Fortunately, I know of no holder who has ever been jailed for fudging on the application, as long as the box was never used for any fraudulent purpose. Hopefully, after filling out the form truthfully, you will then soon move. I am not a lawyer but as I understand it, failing to inform the post office of a move is not a criminal offense. If they ever find out—which is unlikely—they will almost certainly just close your box.

IF YOU SIMPLY CANNOT MOVE, EVER

You might consider renting a cheap apartment on a month-by-month basis, and live there just long enough to rent a box and have that address checked out. Then move back home, but *keep those rent receipts.*

OTHER OPTIONS FOR RECEIVING MAIL AT A PO BOX

Might you have a friend or relative with the same last name? If he or she is agreeable, you could receive mail in their box. Most postal employees have more important duties than to check the first names of everyone in a family.

Another suggestion is to open the box in the name of a limited liability company. *Example:* Your name is Abraham Goldstein but you wish to establish a new identity under the name of Robert Johnson. Form an LLC named "Robert Johnson LLC." Then rent a box in your own name (check the box for Residential/Personal Use). There will be a space for other names (currently on the back of PS Form 1093 July 2011), and this is where you list the LLC. Send yourself a few letters from time to time, addressed to "Robert Johnson LLC." After that, there may be no problem in receiving mail in your new name, even though the ending "LLC" is not included.

Or, for total anonymity along with a new name, find someone whose mailbox you can take over. Either they are moving away or are poor enough so that a cash contribution will allow you to take over their box. (Naturally, you will send *their* mail on to whatever address they later give you.)

Use this person's basic name—with a slight alteration—as if it were your own. For instance, if the box holder's name is José L. Hernandez, just change the first name to Joe, or the middle initial to R. Or, if you are determined to use a different name—say, Veronica Victoria, slowly work your way through the series below, sending letters to this box number and addressed to:

1. Veronica Victoria, c/o José Hernandez
2. V. Victoria & J. Hernandez
3. Victoria & Hernandez
4. V. Victoria

My experience has been that—in many cases—after six months, mail in whatever name will be delivered to the box. When time comes for paying the annual fee, do not of course show up at the counter. Mail in a money order with the name "José L. Hernandez" as the sender.

Here's one more idea: Third-class mail from the previous box holder may still be coming to the box you've just rented. Hmm . . . might that be as good a name as any for your alternate identity? (If you do, however, make sure you never apply for credit in that name, nor use it for any other fraudulent activity. Also, you might check him out on the Internet, to make sure he isn't on something like a sex-offender list!)

FULL DISCLOSURE

I do have a PO box that cannot be tracked to any of my home addresses, but I did not use any of the suggestions above. It is probably not one that you can ever use, but here's what happened:

A friend who lived in the United States for many years decided to return to Mexico. Before she left, I had her go to the local post office and add the name "JJ Luna." Theoretically I should have had to send some ID with her, but as I suspected, they didn't bother to ask. I then exchanged some cash for her two keys, and off she went. I send test letters in my name to the box once in a while, and they are always delivered.

The only persons who know about this address are a few of my consulting clients. They had to send me some confidential information, and short of a personal courier, first-class mail is the best way to send it.

COMMERCIAL MAIL-RECEIVING AGENCIES (CMRAS)

ADVANTAGES

The biggest advantage of having a box number with a private agency is that they will receive mail from private couriers and packages from UPS and FedEx. Also:

- You will have a street address, which in some cases is necessary.
- You can often call in while traveling to have your mail sent on.
- They are often open longer, and/or more days, than a U.S. post office.

DISADVANTAGES

- You will have to sign a "Private Mailbox (PMB) Rental Agreement" that includes a sea of small print. Next, if you are in the United States, you will have to fill out and sign the dreaded PS Form 1583a (June 2011). If an agent at the CMRA does not witness your signature, then it must be notarized.
- You will be required to furnish two forms of identification. Item 10 says that a photocopy of your picture "may be retained by postmaster or designee for verification."
- All major CMRA addresses are kept in commercial databases. This will block your efforts to use such an address on your driver's license or for any other official use. Also, if you order over the Internet, many firms will refuse ship to such an address.

POSSIBLE REMEDIES FOR PRIVATE BOXES

- Rent the box, then *move*, without telling the CMRA.
- Choose a mom-and-pop operation with a single outlet. This address may not show up in national databases, and if you "forget" to add your box number once in a while, they should still—being small and thus recognizing customer names—be able to give you your mail.

SUMMARY

If you do not plan to go beyond Level One security, get a private box at one of the CMRAs and have all your mail sent there. Even if they have your home address on file, it will not be given out indiscriminately to the general public.

For advanced security, however, I strongly suggest you avoid CMRAs. Instead, if at all possible, obtain a PO box that does not connect you with your present home address. Use this box number for:

- Personal mail from relatives and friends
- Bank statements
- Telephone, insurance, and utility bills
- Social Security and Medicare (if applicable)
- Any other strictly personal mail

For everything else—and especially if you receive mail in other names, use a private, alternate street address. This "ghost" address is the subject of the next chapter.

QUESTIONS & ANSWERS

Can I use a PO box or a CMRA street address when I open a bank account?

Although your bank statements can be mailed to either a PO box or a CMRA address, they will ask for your home address. Perhaps you will be able to use the address of a close relative. Otherwise, see the next chapter about obtaining a ghost street address.

When I recently renewed my driver's license, I gave them my address at The UPS Store but without the box number. They didn't say anything, so should I tell my friends to do the same?

Absolutely not. One of my readers went through this process. "I obtained a new driver's license using The UPS Store's address," he says. "I had to sign an affidavit stating that this was my address. Last night I went to a nightclub that uses an ID scanner. When my card was swiped, I looked to see what appeared on the screen. Much to my nonamusement, my actual address was on the screen, instead of the address on my driver's license. I would have to guess—as you have stated—that the DMV knew that the new address that I gave them was a mail drop and not an actual residence. Then, somehow, they pulled up my real address and entered it!"

Can I rent a PO box with a single visit?

Post office employees are not consistent. Some of my readers report getting a box on the first visit by showing ID with their home address. Others, however, have had an experience such as this: "I went to the post office to rent a box. They told me I had to fill out the form and they would then verify the information. After that, they said they would mail me a letter. I would then have to take that letter back to the post office and only then could I obtain a box."

Can I open a PO box without showing my driver's license (which is from another state)?

Normally, yes. Use your passport and, if asked for a second piece of ID, use a current lease, a mortgage, a voter or vehicle registration card, or a home or vehicle insurance policy. One senior citizen writes:

> The clerk used my credit card (she did not know it was canceled) as the second ID. She wrote down my credit card number on the application. Another clerk told her that it was illegal to write the number down. She scribbled it out and said she had gotten yelled at last week by her boss for not writing down the second ID. She then commented that she had never used anything but a license before.

> *Note:* Form 1583A specifically excludes credit cards as identifications.

5

HOW TO OBTAIN YOUR OWN "GHOST" ADDRESS

In the context of this book, a *ghost address* refers to a future address you will use that is not in any database as a CMRA, and has no connection to where you really live. Although I will usually speak of this new address in the singular, you may wish to have multiple ghost addresses. In my own case, I use two U.S. PO boxes, three ghost addresses in North America, and two more here in Spain's Canary Islands. (If you ever happen to vacation in the Canary Islands, don't bother trying to track me down. You could grow old and die before you succeed.)

A PARTIAL LIST WHERE ALTERNATE ADDRESSES WILL BE USED

It is assumed you will use a PO box for personal mail, bank statements, and telephone, insurance, and utility bills. Some items on the following list may also be suitable for using your PO box number.

1. The Internal Revenue Service.
2. Your driver's license.
3. All licenses for your pets (a PI's favorite search).
4. Hunting and fishing licenses.
5. Your voter's registration (if any).
6. Any membership records, such as with your church.
7. Your doctor, dentist, and chiropractor.
8. Your attorney and your accountant.
9. All limited liability companies (LLCs) used to title vehicles and real estate.
10. Cable TV. (Another PI favorite! Make certain it's under another name.)

HOW TO SET UP YOUR OWN GHOST ADDRESS

Shortly after the publication of the first edition of this book, questions began arriving at my Web site, *www.howtobeinvisible. com*. Although the most numerous were about how best to use a limited liability company, the toughest questions had to do with obtaining a ghost address. As you will soon learn, getting your own ghost address may involve major effort, but I assure you that if you do make the effort, *you will never regret it.*

OLDER OFFICE BUILDING

Another reader found a ghost address by locating an older office building that had several floors that needed renovation and had no tenants. All the offices on those empty floors had mail slots in the doors. Even better, the building had multiple entrances on different streets and residential apartments on the upper floors.

The owner was suspicious at first about the idea of renting an office for its mail slot, even after the reader explained that he was often away from home and didn't want neighbors picking up his mail. The owner wanted to know what was wrong with the usual solution: a post-office box.

"Some of it's from FedEx," I explained, "so a PO box won't work." This answer satisfied him. I was able to rent a space on a handshake agreement for $25 per month. The office staff doesn't know my real name or address and my rent bill comes right to my mail slot. It is on an empty floor so it would be difficult for anyone to keep a close watch on it.

CHARITY MISSION

Says Joanne, thirty-two, from Ohio:

Charity missions, like the Salvation Army, often have people stay there for extended periods. They accept mail for residents so they can get jobs, welfare, etc. I told the supervisor that I travel a lot in and out of town and asked him if I could use the address for my personal business and gave him a $50 donation. Now, you could have someone else *say* they are you, do the same thing I did, and have a great layer of protection (no cameras in those places, either).

SMALL MOTEL

Another reader writes:

I've obtained ghost addresses at various independently run mom-and-pop motels. I have found that if I dress well, many of these proprietors are very sympathetic to my situation, provided I am willing to pay them something for the service. The nice

thing about this method is that you have a street address with
no added room number, and of course it's very private. (Cheapo
motels don't often have cameras, either.)

SMALL-TOWN PASTOR

The following is taken from an e-mail received from a young
man in northern California who claims to have almost memorized *How to Be Invisible:*

> I recently moved out into a small country town, away from any
> large city. Knowing that people are friendlier in small towns,
> and the effect a small donation of cash money can have, I found
> my answer for a third ghost address.
>
> There's a small country church maybe a mile from where I
> am moving to. I stopped by and struck up a conversation with
> the pastor. I simply talked to him about the town, adjustments
> I am making from big city life to small town living . . . made
> small talk, really. I told him that I may occasionally order a
> package to be delivered, but I thought the delivery service driver
> "may get lost on some of these back roads." I asked the pastor if
> we could work something out for me to order packages and have
> them sent to the church address instead of mine "thinking it
> would be easier to find a church than where I am."
>
> The pastor laughed out loud, and said several folks in the
> town have things shipped to the church! Since he's a minister
> and into helping people, he said he saw no problem with it, and
> I offered a few bucks if this could be an ongoing thing. Again, *he
> was very agreeable, and my small donation to the church no doubt
> helped his good cheer* [italics added]. He made it crystal clear my
> package would be safe and sound until I would be able to come
> and pick it up. The pastor has a name for me. It's the name I use
> when ordering something, but not my true name. Best part is, *I
> showed him no ID.*

Who's going to think about seeing what's in a small, un-marked box being shipped to a church?

ALTERNATIVE SOURCES FOR A GHOST ADDRESS

Check the Yellow Pages for "Office Services," "Bookkeeping," etc. Don't call them, go in person. Discuss whatever services they offer, and then, as you're leaving, imitate the late Peter Falk in the old *Columbo* shows:

"Oh, *by the way*, do you happen to accept mail here for any of your clients?" If they do not, move on. If, however, they say, "Well, only for three or four . . ." see if they will take you on. If they agree, you can almost certainly be added to their list with-out showing ID. These small services sort mail by name alone, without a box number added. The ideal address is one on a street that also has private residences—the type of street address you will need for such things as car insurance or a library card.

SHOULD YOU ALLOW ANYONE AT YOUR GHOST ADDRESS TO KNOW WHERE YOU LIVE?

Only you can answer that question. Hopefully, when you made the arrangements, you gave an address other than your own, and no telephone number. However, have they gotten to know you? Do they recognize your car? If so, might they have seen it in front of your home? What follows is a chilling example of what unfortunately goes on all too often, not only at commercial mail drops, but even at some of the ghost addresses.

Sally Overstreet (not her actual name) is a newspaper re-porter who has twice moved to avoid an ex-lover who has been stalking her for years. Unknown to Sally, her stalker is now working with a Level Three private investigator.

The PI shows up at her new address. He is wearing a UPS uniform and carries a box addressed to Sally Overstreet. The return address is that of a major New York publisher. The supposed UPS man says he must pick up a certified check for $200 before leaving the box. The next day is a Saturday—or a holiday—and the UPS man insists the box is something Ms. Overstreet has to have *today*. Could the folks at the new address kindly tell him where Ms. Overstreet can be reached? How about a telephone number? Where does she work, maybe the box can be delivered there?

This ruse often works, which is why it remains so popular. The PI's uniform need not appear to be from the UPS. Perhaps it is from FedEx, Brink's Security, or Flowers "R" Us. The return address and the story that comes with it can be anything. The object is the same, to find anyone at your mailing address that knows how to locate you.

There are two ways to protect yourself from this deception. One is to make sure that no one at your new address knows anything about you. The other is to use persons who, although they know you, will positively protect you. If the latter, then make sure to educate them about the various scams that may be used in an attempt to deceive them.

NOW FOR THE HARD PART

The hardest part of keeping your actual home address a secret is to educate your family to never, ever give out your home address to anyone other than relatives and close friends. And *even then* not always, for *they* may innocently pass on your address to others. Even judges and policemen may have problems within the family.

Geraldine Adams, a private investigator in a southern state, specializes in tracking down corporate burglaries. (A stolen notebook computer with corporate files can fetch up to $75,000.)

She had recently been responsible for a police raid and two arrests and as a result, threats had been made on her life. Both she and her husband Tom, a self-employed accountant, took these threats seriously. They sold their home in the suburbs and moved to a new and supposedly secret apartment in the city. They also changed banks and used a telephone answering service for receiving mail. One day Geraldine returned home and was stunned to find in the mail a box of new checks that her husband had ordered from the local bank. Imprinted on every check was their *new home address*. (She destroyed the checks, said some unkind words to her husband, and ordered new checks from Checks in the Mail.)

Mateo, a police detective in Miami, was hated by innumerable bad guys he'd helped put away. For that reason, he was obsessive about keeping his home address secret. One day, while he was at work, his pregnant wife started to hemorrhage. When she could not locate her husband, she called 911. An ambulance took her to the emergency room and when asked, rather than give their ghost address, she gave her actual home address. (For what she *could* have done, see the section "**Calls to 911**" in chapter 10.)

A month later, as a result of his wife's indiscretion, Mateo sold their home and moved.

YOUR HOUSE NUMBER

There may be some local laws about displaying house numbers but if so, I have never known it to be enforced. The reason we do not display a number on our house, much less give anyone the number, is that eventually *someone will write it down*. Then they may use the address to send a thank-you note and the mailperson will discover (1) who lives at this address, and (2) that there is no mailbox.

A friend of ours did let both the mailbox and the number remain on a house he purchased. He neglected to warn a visiting aunt that he never received mail at home. At Christmastime, she sent him a gift subscription to *Robb Report* in his real name, of course, and with his true street address!

If you delete the number on your house but still need to have others find it, here's a little trick. If guests are coming, tell them that once they pass a certain landmark or cross street, "Watch for a house on the right with a pink flamingo on the lawn." (Don't forget to go out and plant the bird before they arrive. Extract it after they leave. They may never find the place again.)

A UNIQUE SOLUTION TO HIDING YOUR HOME ADDRESS

I have a cartoon tacked on my office wall that shows a middle-aged couple in their living room, dressed to go out. The front door is open, and four large suitcases are sitting in the entrance. The husband is pouring gasoline on the carpet. The wife, who holds a can of gasoline in her left hand, is standing along one wall, talking to their daughter on the telephone. She says, "Oh, that sounds lovely, dear, but I'm afraid your father and I have already made plans." Although arson is not recommended, the following solution to hiding your home address is.

I learned this one from a FEMA (Federal Emergency Management Agency) agent I met, while staying in a motel that was near a flooded area. Some years ago he bought a $98,995 motor home under another name, and *did not license it.* (He thus saved not only the license fees and road tax, but an $8,513.57 sales tax as well.) For $12 he got a fifteen-day permit to move it to a rural location in another state. From time to time he moves it, each time getting a temporary permit. Try to find out where *this* agent actually lives!

QUESTIONS & ANSWERS

I am a single mother who is having a hard time setting up a ghost address. Everyone is suspicious. How can I get around this?

Arrive in a new luxury car (borrowed or rented, if necessary). Dress well, perhaps in a skirt and sweater rather than jeans, and smile. Have a good reason ready, such as that you are being stalked by some dirty old man. If that doesn't work, show up with an attorney at your side who will support your well-rehearsed story.

Tip #1: If the person you are going to see is a woman, bring a male attorney. If it's a man, bring a female attorney.

Tip #2: In some cases, if money is not available for an attorney, a friend from out of town could come along to pose as one. Don't try this one, however, unless the friend can truly dress, act, and speak like an attorney. According to some sources, anyone can *say* he or she is an attorney as long as no fraud is involved, but try this at your own risk. Alternatives are to bring with you a banker, a doctor, or your tax accountant.

We do use our home address on our tax returns, but isn't that information confidential?

Louis Mitzel Jr., a former special agent and intelligence officer with the U.S. Department of State and a prolific author, tells the story of Lee Willis, a lowly clerk with the Internal Revenue Service (IRS). Willis had been stalking his ex-girlfriend for sixteen months. She thought she was safe because her home address was kept secret, her telephone number was kept secret, and she made sure her friends and neighbors kept a lookout for the stalker.

Although 56,000 IRS employees have access to taxpayer files, Willis was not one of them. He did, however, persuade a co-worker to illegally run a search for him. The ex-girlfriend was filing her tax returns under her true address. Willis raced to her apartment building. The lobby was locked, but he pressed all the buzzers and one of the neighbors let him in. At the last moment, the girl discovered he was in the building, called the police, and they arrested him. When they then searched Willis's car, they found a stun gun, rope, latex gloves, duct tape, and a knife.

Does that answer your question? Let's say each of the 56,000 IRS employees with access to the records has 5 close friends, and each of these friends has 5 close friends of his own. Are you willing to bet your life that not one of these 1.4 million persons would ever commit an illegal act, or coerce another into doing so?

Is it okay to put my true home address on the bags I check, when traveling by air?

Not if you value your privacy! If a piece of luggage goes astray, the address will be entered into the airline's database and your name will then be tied forever to your home address.

My son-in-law used to travel around the world on business and *never* checked luggage—a practice I do my best to follow. But otherwise, put the address of a friend—or that of your CMRA—on the tags.

How can I avoid giving out my daughter's Social Security number, as well as our street address, when she starts school next year?

Privacy in a public school system is nonexistent—simply unachievable. To maintain privacy, you do have two options:

1. A private school.
2. Home schooling (check out www.k12.com).

In our own case, we raised our three children in Spain, at a time when—thanks to Generalissimo Francisco Franco—drugs were simply not available and sex among teenagers was unknown.

We put the kids in a private school (German, with professors from Berlin), and when classes let out, my wife spent the next two hours with them teaching English. Although we took each child out of school at age fifteen, each in turn was better educated than the majority of today's high school graduates, and could speak, read, and write in three languages.

> *Friendly tip:* Raise your children to be self-employed when they leave home, so that their names will never, ever, go into the National Directory for New Hires. And just think of all the money you'll save by not sending them to college! (Like Mark Zuckerberg, I am a university dropout. I don't know about Zuckerberg, but I myself have never regretted dropping out during my senior year, back in the 1940s. Not for a day, an hour, or a minute.)

Says columnist Arnold Ahlert from *Jewish World Review*, October 13, 2011 (italics added):

> Maybe the smartest thing the protesters, and perhaps of lot of other Americans, could do would be to pressure businesses to stop making a college degree the ultimate criterion for getting a job. If one considers where the so-called "best and brightest" among us have taken this country in the last few years, one could make a compelling argument that *a college degree is the most overrated product on the planet.*

REPAIRMEN, HOME DELIVERIES, FEDEX, UPS

George Joseph Phillips, who lives in the 600 block of South "D" Street in Tacoma, Washington, is a photographer. His nightmare began when he called Washington Energy Services Co. to get a new furnace and water heater installed. When work began, an employee spotted some darkroom chemicals and, apparently unfamiliar with darkroom supplies, told his boss he saw chemicals in the home that he felt might be used to manufacture drugs. A company official then notified the police. Please pay more than the usual attention to what followed. According to the headline of an article in a Seattle newspaper "Utility's House Call Became a Nightmare."

> Phillips claims that after the company reported its suspicions to police, a member of the Police Department asked the company to gather information from Phillips's home so police could obtain a search warrant.

> The article goes on to report that the employees—yes, the ones Phillips was paying to install the furnace and water heater—

then took "pictures of the home's interior," and searched through Phillips's personal effects. Further, he suspects *they also searched his computer files* because his computer was broken and beyond repair after the search. Whether or not this was an illegal and unconstitutional search—and I think it was—let's benefit from Philips's experience, shall we? The next time a worker enters *your* home, think beforehand about what could possibly give him a false impression. Then, when you let him in, stick with him.

OBTAINING CONSENT TO ENTER BY DECEPTION

The following is based on information from the January 1994 *F.B.I. Law Enforcement Bulletin*, now in the public domain. The below applies to any home that federal agents would like to search, but for lack of evidence are unable to obtain a warrant.

A van that appears to be from a well-known courier service pulls into your driveway and the driver, with a package in hand, rings your bell. He asks for a certain person and when you say no such person lives at this address, he asks to use your telephone to supposedly "call the company." If you allow him to do it, and if— while in your home—he observes anything that *might* be illegal, he may return within a few hours. This time he'll be with police officers who have a warrant to search your home, based on what the "deliveryman" observed earlier.

You and I are law-abiding persons, with nothing to hide. Nevertheless, why invite strangers into your home? Just say no, and give the location of the nearest pay phone. Or, if you need an excuse, here are two:

- "My husband," says the wife, "told me never to allow strangers into the house when he's not here."
- "All we have is a cell phone and I lent it to my father today."

Sometimes, of course, no warrant is needed, as the following section explains.

COURIER SERVICES SUCH AS FEDEX AND UPS

The only sure way to avoid having someone send you an envelope or a package by courier is to never, ever, let anyone other than your closest friends know where you really live. The result is that, should a uniformed courier show up on your doorstep—or even a clown with balloons!—you automatically *know* that he or she doesn't belong there. In fact, if you see someone coming up the walk—or observe them through the peephole that I hope you have in your door—and do not know them, why open at all? When I was younger, cars were stolen, not hijacked, but improvements in car alarms have brought about a change. The same is starting to be true with house burglaries, now that locks and burglar alarms have improved. Thugs may just ring your doorbell. When you open, they slam their way in. Housejacking started in New York some years ago, then jumped to the West Coast. It may soon be coming to your hometown.

Now then, just in case you consider some of my advice to be extreme—and I confess that many do—I am willing to discuss some options. I don't recommend them, but better half an ounce of prevention than none at all.

HOME DELIVERY

Never allow your true name to be coupled with a delivery to your home. If you feel that it is imperative to have a delivery made to where you really live, *it must not be in your name.* All courier companies keep a national database of names and addresses and countless thousands of their employees can run a search of your name. PIs know this and many have contacts inside these companies.

If, in fact, you have *ever* received a letter or package at your present address under your real name, the only way to protect your privacy is to move. Once this move has been made, then any future delivery must be in another name. When you sign for the delivery, sign your *other* name.

You may get by with no problems doing this, as long as you do not order expensive items from out of state. If you do, however, keep in mind that in states with a sales tax, it is not uncommon for irate neighbors to call the tax department and report that the people next door are buying such-and-such to avoid the state's sales tax. (You do know, do you not, that you are obligated to "voluntarily" pay any local sales tax on merchandise purchased from out of state?)

The logical solution to anonymity with courier services would be to have your parcels come into one of their nearby offices and just pick them up there. Unfortunately, these companies do not employ logic. Whereas they never ask for ID at a private home, they absolutely demand it if you stop by one of their offices to pick anything up. I have argued this point in vain with the various home offices, pointing out that if I send a package in a certain name, I will sign a waiver to the effect that they may deliver to any person asking for it in that name. After all, this is similar to item number 8 on all FedEx labels, which reads: "Release Signature. Sign to authorize delivery without obtaining signature." In fact, if you really wish to remain incognito, have the sender sign on the line for this release and when you see the FedEx truck arrive, do not answer the door.

But do not pick up at their office. I sent an e-mail to the FedEx main office, pleading for permission to send a letter to one of my clients who would not present ID when he picked it up at an office in Memphis. I received this short, but not sweet, reply:

Thank you for your inquiry. FedEx requires a valid consignee name and phone number for shipments that are held for pick-up. More hold for pick-up information can be found on our website.

    Thank you for your interest in FedEx.
Susan Carr
FedEx Webmaster

MAIL DROP PICKUP

Although USPS regulations require that you show picture ID in order to receive mail sent to you as "General Delivery," the commercial mail receiving agencies are apparently not bound by these regulations. So then, even though you have not rented a box at the CMRA, you can normally receive a shipment there in a business name and no ID is necessary. The following is an example of how it works.

Assume I live in Plano, Texas. I wish to have a friend from New York City send me a small box that will not be identified with me in any way. Not by my name, and not by my address. I look up The UPS Store in the Yellow Pages, choose one of the six offices listed, and have my wife make the call. The conversation goes like this:

"Hello, this is Mary Johnson with Triple R Services in New York. I wish to send a small box to your address, for pickup by one of our salesmen traveling through. Will that be satisfactory?"

"No problem—in whose name will it be?"

"We'll just send it to your address in the name of Triple R Services. Anyone that asks for a package in that name can pick it up."

"There is a small pick-up fee, of course . . ."

"No problem."

I then call my friend, who ships the package. The following

week I stop by, pay the fee, and pick up the box. (I have my wife make these calls so that when I ask for the box, the manager does not recognize my rather odd accent and connect it with the supposed "New York" caller.) Or, I can send anyone else around on my behalf, anyone at all.

ROBBERS MAY IMPERSONATE THE POLICE

If no one knows where you live, it is extremely unlikely that police will ever show up at your door. If, therefore, you see what appear to be policemen coming up your walk, if you have even the slightest doubt about them, do not open the door. Call the police department or even 911 on your cell phone, to check them out.

Some years ago, two men who identified themselves as police officers entered a home in a Los Angeles suburb with their guns drawn and tied up the couple who lived there. Both men wore dark clothing and caps with the word POLICE on the brow. They then stole $1,000 in cash and a laptop computer.

"Unfortunately, this happens too often," said LAPD spokesman Lieutenant Anthony Alba, "but generally on the east side or the south side of town, where recent immigrants might not be familiar with our law-enforcement officials. This one's a bit different." He referred to the fact that the victims were from a relatively quiet street in a predominantly middle-class neighborhood.

Later, two Los Angeles men suspected of committing more than thirty home-invasion robberies were arrested on suspicion of several theft, assault, and drug crimes. At a widely publicized press conference, police displayed more than one hundred items confiscated from the suspects' home, including night-vision goggles, official Los Angeles police badges, handcuffs, five handguns, a sawed-off shotgun, an assault rifle, and hundreds of rounds of ammunition.

* * *

In summary, a ghost address will give you not only protection but peace of mind as well. No longer will you have to wonder who is coming to your door. If it is not someone you recognize, then—since no one else has this address—they have no business there. The postman? Ignore him! Woman dressed in a FedEx uniform? Ignore her! Two or three guys in leather jackets? Don't even *think* of answering your door! (See how easy it is, once you eliminate all traces of your home address?)

PIZZA DELIVERIES

You may feel confident in calling in an order for pizza, because you give them a different name. However, it's safer never to have pizza delivered to your home under any name, and here's why.

Suppose all a PI has to work with is your unlisted number (567-1234) and he's after your name and especially your home address (677 Camino Privado). From the telephone prefix, he will know what city you live in. His next step will be to call every major pizza delivery company in town, because he knows that in most areas these companies log the numbers of their customers for quicker future orders. The following is what happens:

PI: I need a delivery.

Pizza Place: What's your phone number?

PI: 567-1234.

Pizza Place: Are you still at 677 Camino Privado?

PI: Yeah, same address. Oh, hang on a sec . . . wait . . . something's come up . . . Guess I'll have to cancel for now. Sorry!

Didn't take the man very long to get your home address, did it? And with the address, it won't take long to get your name. Remember, never receive anything at your home—no mail, no packages, no courier deliveries, *nada. That means no pizza, either.*

IF YOUR HOME ADDRESS IS ALREADY KNOWN, MOVE

I suspect that for most of you readers, your home address is readily available. In addition to the regular mail, FedEx or UPS has also delivered there, and perhaps pizza as well. By far the best move you can make to protect your privacy, then, is to do just that. Move.

Mexican journalist Fernando Balderas and his wife Yolanda Figueroa wrote a book called *The Boss of the Gulf: The Life and Capture of Juan Garcia Abrego.* The book was dedicated to Mexico's federal attorney general, Antonio Lozano Gracia. At that time Fernando and Yolanda lived, with their children Patricia, Paul, and Fernando Jr., in an attractive home in an upscale neighborhood in Mexico City. Although nothing in the book appeared to warrant retribution, it did discuss Mexico's drug lords and revealed bribery in high circles. What happened next is described in a *USA Today* article:

> MEXICO CITY—Police found journalist Fernando Balderas, his author wife, Yolanda Figueroa, and their three children, ages 18, 13, and 8, bludgeoned to death in their beds last week . . . a brutal murder that shocked even hardened residents. Adding to the intrigue: Police say the family was probably murdered Tuesday night, a day after President Ernesto Zedillo fired Mexico's federal attorney general Antonio Lozano Gracia, to whom the Figueroa's book was dedicated.

I suspect that the Balderas family did indeed think about moving, but then decided it would be too much trouble.

ANOTHER EXAMPLE OF SOMEONE WHO FAILED TO MOVE

Washington state resident Elizabeth Reed, twenty-eight, dated Anthony Nitsch Jr., thirty-two, for about two months. Then, concerned about his drinking, Elizabeth told Anthony the relationship was over. When she stopped taking his calls, he became angry and began stalking and harassing her.

Anonymous packages arrived at her home, one with a dead skunk, another with a sex toy and an obscene message. Strange items began to appear in her yard. Someone disconnected her heat pump fuse box and defecated on it. Her new fiancé came to visit her and when he returned to his car he discovered the tires had been slashed.

Two years passed. Elizabeth continued to live *at the same address*. She went to a judge and sought a restraining order against Anthony. The judge refused to grant it because Elizabeth could not prove Anthony was the person who was harassing her. Then, on a warm Monday night in early June, Anthony cut the telephone line that led into her home, He broke in, threatened her, and fired one shot at her from a .40-caliber handgun.

The ending of this story is not as sad as might normally be the case. I have before me the Tacoma, Washington, *News Tribune* dated June 5. The headline on page 3 reads: "Intruder Who Was Shot Held for $500,000 Bail." Although Elizabeth Reed had failed to move away, she was armed and ready. Nitsch missed. Reed did not. "Nitsch remained in serious condition Wednesday," continues the article, "at Harborview Medical Center with five gunshot wounds to his chest."

TROUBLE OR NOT, MOVING IS BETTER

In the late fall of 2011, I received an urgent message from Keith, one of my readers who lives in a small city in Illinois. His best friend, Vic, had been on a major drug bust a few weeks earlier.

When the leader—I'll call him Pancho—burst out of a back room to attack, Vic dropped him to the floor with the butt of his shotgun. Pancho and his confederates went to jail. That was not, however, the end of the story.

"Last Thursday," wrote Keith, "Vic learned that there was an offer on the street—$50,000 cash for the murder of Vic and his family. The other officers checked with informants who confirmed it. None of them claimed to know who was behind it but it has to be Pancho!"

As this book is being written, I am preparing to meet with both Vic and one of the other cops who's fearful that Vic may not be the only one targeted. Both know that they must move, fast, and pull their kids out of public school as well. They plan to enroll the children in a private school under altered last names.

QUESTIONS & ANSWERS

Can a bounty hunter legally break into my home?

If you ever post bail via a bondsman, and fail to show up in court, then the answer is, *Yes indeed*. There have been a number of articles and programs about this fact. As reported on the CBS program *60 Minutes*, a bounty hunter—unlike the police—can search whatever he likes without a warrant. He can break down doors, read mail, power up your laptop, check out your smartphone, copy any keys he finds, whatever.

The justification for all this is that anyone arranging bail through a bondsman signs a contract, and the bounty hunter is merely fulfilling the fine print in said contract. So if any of you readers ever forfeit bail, you'd better make sure your home address is *really* private.

A more likely danger is that, knowingly or unknowingly, you invite someone into your home that has forfeited bail. This might be a relative, a close friend, maybe even your brother, or grown son or daughter. You might wish to give this some thought, the next time a certain someone "stops by." In some cases, there is a danger even in *knowing* the persons the bounty hunters are after.

One person interviewed on the *60 Minutes* program told of a couple being held and grilled for eleven hours by bounty hunters intent on getting enough information to track down someone this couple knew.

If someone pounds on your door and yells "Special agent!" you are about to meet one or more bounty hunters (who prefer to call themselves "bail recovery agents") in person. Do not be fooled by the fact they may wear uniforms, carry badges, and at first glance appear to be with the FBI or the ATF. Or, they may get you to open the door by dressing as an employee of UPS, FedEx, or the U.S. Postal Service. In one case, the hunters determined that one particular tough quarry—who was wise to all normal ruses—had a young daughter whose birthday was coming up. They waited until that day, then sent in a clown with balloons. He passed muster with the closed-circuit video, the door was opened, and you can guess the rest.

What about the cleaning lady or the carpet cleaner?

At the very least, use someone that your friends have used for years and will recommend without reservations. However, if you have deep secrets to protect, this precaution may not be enough. PIs have been known to offer serious money to obtain trash from a home office before papers have been shredded.

My next suggestion may be worth far more to you than the price you paid for this book. Employ only longtime members of Jehovah's Witnesses. Unlike the mainstream religions, virtually no Witnesses are in jail anywhere unless (as in many countries)— they are there for their faith.

These people would rather die than cheat, use drugs, steal, or accept a bribe to sell their employer out. For this reason, Witnesses do up to 80 percent of the nightly janitorial work in office buildings in major American cities, and are much in demand for nighttime janitorial work in clinics (due to drugs being present). They also do the cleaning in many upscale homes and mansions where security is paramount.

The Witnesses often have no objections to working late at night or very early in the morning, because this gives them time for their ministry during the day. Another plus is that they'll work on December 25, January 1, July 4, or any other national holiday.

Although they call their meeting places "Kingdom Halls," you can find them in the Yellow Pages under "Churches." Over the years we've learned that the best time to call a Kingdom Hall is at 6:45 p.m. on a Tuesday, or 9:45 a.m. on a Sunday. (This is fifteen minutes before a meeting is about to start.) Ask to speak to one of the "elders." If they are busy, leave your number and have them call back. When an elder comes on the line, do not call him an "elder," and don't use a title such as pastor or reverend—they do not use titles. Just explain what you need and add that you prefer a worker who is a "pioneer." This is the term Witnesses use for those who put a certain minimum number of hours in their Bible-teaching work. They cannot be pioneers unless they have an excellent reputation both within and without their congregation.

There is no reason to be embarrassed about calling. Businessmen often call Kingdom Halls to ask about hiring one of their members for some job. If you are hiring a Witness crew for offices where secrets *must* be protected, explain your circumstances to them. Instruct them never to leave the trash in the building's Dumpster. Instead, they are to take the trash with them and dispose of it in some other way. Also, stress the importance of calling you immediately if anyone approaches them and even *hints* at being interested in your trash.

Although they may charge you more than the lowest-bidder

types, trust me on this one: It will be money well spent. And not to worry—they won't preach to you while on the job.

What about letting a babysitter into our home?

I agree with authors and speakers such as Dr. Laura Schlessinger who warn you to never use a babysitter other than Grandma.

Even if you ignore this advice, you may later start to harbor vague fears. If so, set up a voice-activated recorder with multiple pickup microphones. You may hear phone calls, boyfriends coming to visit, or sounds of child abuse. A better solution is to install a nanny-cam and see what goes on in living color. Perhaps she is checking out your computer or going through your drawers!

Actually, however, if you suspect the sitter may need electronic surveillance, your fears are probably right. Better to call Grandma, take the baby with you, or stay home yourself.

UNTRACEABLE TRASH, ANONYMOUS UTILITIES

One of my PI friends reports getting the following information about a couple with two teens. It took him less than a week. None of the information came from an informant or from the Internet.

- The name of their doctor and the information that the father was buying Viagra.
- Someone in the family was consuming a lot of cheap whiskey.
- The son was working for minimum wage at a hamburger joint.
- The family was behind on their phone bills, due to lengthy calls to Spain.

So where did the information come from? From their trash. Once set on the curb, it's fair game for anyone! And such items as empty pill bottles, paycheck stubs, bank statements, telephone bills, magazines, and want ads that are circled in a newspaper can reveal amazing amounts of information.

CAN YOU SOLVE THIS MYSTERY?

A bilingual private investigator in San Jose, California, takes a call from a law firm in San Diego. They wish to locate a certain Victor R. in order to serve a subpoena in a civil lawsuit. They have only two pieces of information:

1. Victor, who was born in Ameca, Jalisco, is staying with friends from his hometown. They live "somewhere" near Lake Tahoe, on the California–Nevada border.
2. Victor has a younger brother named Fernando who rents a one-bedroom unit in a sixty-four-unit apartment complex in San Jose. However, the PI is *not* to contact Fernando because if he does, Fernando will tip off his brother.

Worse, the lawyers want fast results and yet they put a limit on what the PI may spend. If he needs any helpers, he will have to use slave labor. The intrepid PI takes the job, despite the following drawbacks:

- If Victor is with friends, there is no way to track him down via rental agreement, telephone, or utilities.
- There are more than 10,000 Latinos in the Lake Tahoe area and nearly 80 percent of them come from the same place: Ameca, Jalisco (Mexico).
- A quick check shows that there is no landline telephone at Fernando's apartment.

Our resolute PI is on the job that very evening, prepared for action. What he wants is every bit of trash that leaves Fernando's apartment for the next thirty days. He observes that there are two large Dumpsters near the entrance of the parking lot, and learns that they are dumped between 3 and 4 a.m. every day. There is no uniformity in the bags the residents are using. Some are paper, some are white plastic bags from the supermarkets, and some are large black trash bags. The PI knows of a Guatemalan family where three teenagers are desperate for work, any kind of work, even diving into Dumpsters. If you wish to play detective, see if you can answer this question:

How will his Guatemalan friends know which garbage belongs to Fernando?

Okay, check your answer with what happened next. Late one evening, the PI goes from door to door, calling at each of the sixteen apartments that were on Fernando's floor. He wears a uniform with a name tag and presents each renter with a free supply of thirty trash bags, speaking Spanish or English as the occasion warrants.

"This is part of an experiment by our company," he says with a disarming smile. "The idea is to see if these extra-strong bags will cause less spillage when our trucks unload at the processing plant. If you and your neighbors use these bags for the next thirty days, we may continue to furnish them at no charge."

A young, pregnant woman answers the door at Fernando's apartment. He gives her the pitch and hands her the bags.

"Muchas gracias," she says.

Then the three Guatemalans got their assignment. They are to take turns drifting past the Dumpsters both morning and evening, checking to see if there is a bag from Fernando's apartment. For every bag they bring in, the PI pays them $20 cash. If he finds what he is looking for, there will be a $100 bonus.

In the next two weeks, they bring in eight bags, and two days later they bring in the bag that pays a $100 bonus—Fernando has a smartphone and he's tossed the statement in the trash after tearing it into tiny pieces. Pieced together with tape, the statement shows six long-distance calls to the same number at Zephyr Cove on the Nevada side of Lake Tahoe. That's all it takes to track down Victor, at a cost of $280 to the kids and $96 for the bags.

Have you have already guessed how the kids knew which bags to pick up? At fifteen doors, the PI gave away dark green bags. At Fernando's door, he handed over dark blue bags.

To paraphrase the late Johnnie Cochran:

If it can be read,
Then you must shred.

WHAT YOUR TRASH REVEALS ABOUT YOU

Trash is not the remains of food. That is garbage. Trash is everything else. Unfortunately, the two may be mixed unless it is coming from an office building. Trash is to a detective what a gold nugget is to a prospector. Just imagine what investigators would have learned about *you* and *your* family if they had secretly gone through your trash for the last ninety days. We shall assume they started with a blank sheet, having no idea as to the occupants of your home. To put a picture together, they would have watched for any of the items in the following list. If there were any items that you had merely torn up (rather than using a shredder), they would have put the pieces back together.

- Bank statements with your name, address, account number, and balance.
- Telephone bills revealing your number.
- Utility and other bills, showing the name and address you use for those.
- Credit card statements and receipts, invoices, ATM receipts.
- Paycheck and/or money order stubs.
- Empty bottles from prescription medicine, with your doctor's name.

- Personal and business letters; all address labels.
- Scraps of paper revealing a phone number or e-mail address.
- Beer cans, wine, and liquor bottles.
- Anything to indicate drug use, including triangular scraps of paper.
- Itemized grocery and pharmacy slips, for evidence of alcohol, illness, condoms, birth control pills, or anything to indicate homosexual activity.
- Classified ads from newspapers, to see if anything is circled.
- Magazines, travel brochures, or anything that would indicate interest in weapons or strange practices.

What else can you think of, in your particular case? Or that of your friends, relatives, or even your children?

Do you have a weekly arrangement for a woman to come in and clean? Does she have access to the trash?

If you work in an office, who handles the trash? Did you know that janitors are sometimes bribed to turn trash from a specific office over to private investigators or government agents?

Mostly likely, if you do everything else right, no one will be able to sift through your trash because they cannot find you in the first place. But *if they do* (perhaps by following you home), then make sure all papers have been shredded and that there is nothing further to be revealed from your trash. (Empty prescription bottles, whiskey bottles, and other nonshreddable items are best tossed in a Dumpster far away.)

UTILITIES

By utilities I mean the companies that furnish electricity, garbage pickup, water and sewer connections, and natural or propane gas.

(Telephones will be discussed in chapter 10.) Never give your true name—much less your Social Security number or date of birth!—to a utility company, nor to any other private company that will furnish a service at your actual residence.

Rather, if you own your home in the name of a limited liability company (see chapter 15), give each company the name of the LLC and insist that the name in the company database is in the name of the LLC only. In fact, do not give them your own name under any condition. Try a fictitious one, or use your wife's maiden name. Even then, this should just be her middle initial plus last name. Do not furnish her Social Security number or date of birth.

A quick-and-dirty method of setting up the utility accounts on short notice is to use a nominee (proxy), someone who will act on your behalf (see chapter 13.) Usually, the utility company will demand a cash deposit in lieu of being able to check your credit by using your Social Security number. Fine, give them a money order or a bank check for the deposit. It will be returned to you after one year of timely payments. Make sure that the bills *never* come to your home address. Give them your "ghost" address (see chapter 5), explaining that (a) you do not have a mailbox at the street address, and (b) all bills are paid from your "business" (ghost) address.

What has been accomplished? Just this: If a private investigator—acting on behalf of a stalker or working with a law firm or insurance company—starts searching for you, one of the first places he will check (after cable TV) will be the utility companies. If your name is in any database, the PI will obtain the address. But as long as your name never shows up, the search will be in vain.

QUESTIONS & ANSWERS

We have a small business that deals with top-secret information. How can we make sure that trash taken from our office building at night does not, under any circumstances whatsoever, fall into the hands of a private investigator from one of our competitors?

First on the list is to cross-shred everything. Then, give the job to the class of janitors recommended previously. Here is an additional suggestion, in case you do not want anyone to even *read* what may be lying open on a desk.

In larger cities, there are congregations of Jehovah's Witnesses who speak other languages besides English, such as Spanish, Russian, Tagalog, Vietnamese, Arabic, Mandarin Chinese, French, Hindi, Japanese, Albanian, Polish, Portuguese, Greek, Punjabi, Hmong, and—in California—Quechua. Communication may be a problem, but if the workers speak a little if any English, that may be a plus. If fact, if a PI tries to bribe a worker who speaks only Albanian or Chinese Mandarin, best of luck!

What's the best kind of a shredder to use?

A year ago I sent out a mass e-mail to those on my privacy list, warning my readers to use only cross-cut shredders because strip shredders may not be as secure as they thought. (This was because some PIs now hire retired persons to put strips together using a special clipboard tool.)

I received some interesting feedback from my readers. The best came from Hamlet in Washougal, Washington. A warning for us all!

> My mother (bless her soul) once shredded an important medical receipt. Upon discovering her mistake, she took the pieces and, while watching the Larry King show, put the puzzle back together. She was so proud of her work when she finished!

YOUR SOCIAL SECURITY NUMBER AND DATE OF BIRTH

In 1973, George Norman left Denver, Colorado, in a borrowed car. He was skipping out on an impending two-year prison sentence for embezzling some $500,000 from the now-defunct Rocky Mountain Bank. Over the years he ran this "starter money" into $50 million by legal means, dabbling in oil in Houston and starting software companies in Oregon and Utah.

Although he knew that U.S. marshals were after him, rather than move to Mexico or Canada he stayed in the United States, relying on alternate names to protect him. Some of the names he used were George Larson, Max Morris, George Irving, Frick Jensen, Gunner Isoz, J. Blankman, and Dr. James Hill.

Had private parties been employing detectives to pursue him, the money would have run out before many years had passed. However, with government agents, money does not run out. Twenty-three years passed before Norman, for whatever reason, felt compelled to give out a Social Security number. Rather than use his own, or invent one, he used the number of a person he knew was dead. This Social Security number came up on a government computer as that of Tom Dangelis, red-flagged as George Norman's wife Donna's deceased grandfather! The result was this headline in the Sunday, December 1, 1996, *Los Angeles Times:* "Fugitive Millionaire Nabbed After 23 Years on the Lam."

Yes, Norman needed catching and they caught him. But the point is, privacy isn't only for criminals, it's also desirable for white-hat folks like you and me, and this story certainly illustrates the point about not using someone else's Social Security number. It also tells us, as I say in chapter 1, that when the chips go down for whatever reason, your first priority may be to gain time to sort things out. One way to find that time is to cross a border to the north or south. Even Denver's Deputy U.S. Marshal Bobby Lloyd wondered about this, as indicated in the closing paragraph of the *Los Angeles Times* article:

"A guy with this amount of money," said Lloyd, "why he didn't just leave the country, I don't know."

YOUR DATE OF BIRTH (DOB)

No matter how common your name, you can be quickly identified in a database by coupling either your name *or* your birth date with your address. Keeping your true home address a secret has already been discussed. As for a birth date, I seldom give out any date whatsoever.

For instance, I once stopped in at a shopping mall to have my eyes tested. The doctor's assistant handed me a long form to fill out, asking, among other things, my address, telephone number, Social Security number, and date of birth. I explained that I did not live in the area, did not give out my Social Security number, and my age was "more or less old." No objection was raised. During the exam, the doctor asked me what I did for a living.

"I'm a writer."

"Oh? What do you write?"

"Articles and books about keeping your private life *private*. Which is why I didn't give you a Social Security number nor a date of birth."

"Oh, well," replied the doctor, "except for insurance cases, I don't need that stuff on the form anyway!" (But they don't tell you that when they hand you the form, right?)

My next stop was nearby, at one of those national chains that have optical shops in malls. I picked out the two frames I wanted and the young sales clerk started to fill in the form.

"Address?" she asked.

"No local address, I live in Spain." After a puzzled look, she wrote down the address of the store itself.

"Telephone number?"

"Sorry, no telephone." She wrote down the number of the store.

"Date of birth?"

"Why on earth," I said, "would the purchase of two pairs of glasses require a date of birth?"

"The date of birth is how we identify our customers."

"I do not wish to be identified." Long pause. Then she left it blank. The next question on the form was for a Social Security number but at this point the girl just shrugged and didn't even ask me.

Personally, I enjoy these challenges, but some of my clients do not. In fact, they hate confrontations of any kind. Often, if filling in a form yourself, you can just write "legal age." Another alternative is to give a fictitious month and day, and a year a bit before or after the real one. If you feel obligated to give a date of birth, choose one that is easy to remember, such as a national holiday. Why not make yourself a few years younger at the same time?

YOUR SOCIAL SECURITY NUMBER (SSN)

The Privacy Act of 1974 (Pub. L. 93–579, I section 7) requires that any federal, state, or local government agency that requests your Social Security number (SSN) must tell you four things:

1. Whether disclosure of your SSN is required or optional.
2. What statute or other authority requires this number.
3. How they will use your SSN, once they have it.
4. What will happen if you do not provide them with your SSN.

So if you are asked for your SSN by any federal, state, or local government agency (including any state university that accepts federal funds), look for the Privacy Act Statement. If it isn't there, ask to see it before you give your number.

Since the subject of this book is privacy, not tax evasion, I see no problem in furnishing your SSN to the Internal Revenue Service.

YOUR DRIVER'S LICENSE (DL)

By the time you read this, American and Canadian drivers' licenses will be approaching the level of what in Europe is called a National Identification Card. However, unlike Europe, you are seldom required to show your DL in North America. I believe the only time I've ever had to produce my driver's license has been either at a car rental agency or when pulled over by a cop. All other times, I use my passport for ID.

My one caveat is to do all that is legally possible to avoid having your true home address on your license, just in case some PI has a spy inside the DMV. But other than that, I don't feel there's much of a problem when dealing with government agencies. It's the *private* organizations that can give you industrial-strength depression. The low-level clerk behind the counter expects you to fill out that form *completely*. After all, "everyone else does," and it's "the company policy." So let's consider some of these private agencies or organizations:

YOUR EMPLOYER'S DEMAND FOR YOUR DL, DOB, AND SSN

The ideal employer is you yourself. I have been self-employed since 1958, and I recommend that course to one and all. But if this is not possible for you, then here comes some bad news.

When you work for wages, the IRS requires the employer to get your Social Security number. Often they will ask for it before you're hired, so they can check your credit and criminal (if any) record. Tell them you'll give them your SSN if and when actually hired for the job. If this is not acceptable, ask yourself, "How badly do I want this job?"

If you do take the job, know that your name, address, and Social Security number must by law go into the database for the National Directory of New Hires within twenty calendar days. This applies to virtually every person who is hired in the United States. The only wiggle room here is with the address. Do all within your power to give your employer only your ghost address. (If you don't yet have one, perhaps you can use the address of a relative who lives in the same area.)

In some cases, you may be able to work as an independent contractor and thus avoid giving out your Social Security number. An independent contractor is someone who works for another person or firm as a separate entity. The details are too complex to go into here, but if you think you might qualify, consult a CPA.

HOSPITALS AND DOCTORS

If you qualify for Medicare *and wish to use it,* you'll need to furnish your true Social Security number. Other than that, I know of no law that requires your SSN to be an ID number. Insurance companies can often be persuaded to use another number in lieu of the SSN. True, the insurance companies do send information to the Medical Information Bureau (MIB), but I've been told the MIB does not use Social Security numbers as identifiers, nor do they report Social Security numbers when making reports.

Remember, when a private investigator has an associate search for your records in the Medical Information Bureau, many identical names may come up. His first choice for picking you out will be your date of birth, and his second choice will be whatever address he may have for you (if any). The very last thing you want on your record is a consultation that indicates a nervous disorder, a psychiatric problem, or a sexually transmitted disease. For these consultations, pay cash and use a false name. Better yet, pop over into Canada or Mexico. If you can afford it, skip Medicare altogether and just pay all bills in cash. No personal information needed for that.

BANKS

If you must have a U.S. bank account, open it in a business name or in the name of another person. When cashing checks, do not use your driver's license for identification. Rather, use your passport because:

- It does not show your Social Security number.
- It does not show any address for you, not even the state or country in which you live.

- Unlike the Department of Motor Vehicles (or whatever name it has in your state), you cannot easily be traced with your passport number.

Occasionally, after presenting my passport, I have been asked for my driver's license. I reply that I do not use my driver's license for ID. In one small town, the bank teller confessed that she had never seen a passport before! I had to point out where the number was, so she could write it on the third-party check I was cashing.

If you do not yet have a passport, apply for one even though you have no intention of traveling to foreign lands. From the time it arrives, this will be the ID to use at all times.

Update: This e-mail came in just as this section was being edited:

> *Yet another big thanks to you for opening my eyes to privacy issues. Because of your book, I finally decided to get a passport as my first step in following your advice. Within just a few months, my father-in-law passed away in Spain and I had to go overseas immediately. Having the passport already was definitely a saving grace. I wouldn't have had it if not for you!*
> —Gail Lucero, Las Vegas, NV

RENTING AN APARTMENT

Apartment managers present one of the greatest challenges a privacy-seeker will ever face. You, on the one hand, wish to keep your rental contract private. The manager, however, has almost certainly had some bad experiences with renters in the past and he is determined not to repeat them. With the escalating amount of identity fraud and the increased security ever since 9/11, most landlords now require:

- Your driver's license (which may be photocopied) and a second piece of identification, such as a credit card.
- Your date of birth.
- The name, address, and telephone number of one or more references, preferably relatives.
- Your Social Security number, so he can check both your credit and a statewide database (i.e., blacklist) of undesirable tenants.
- The name of your employer, your monthly income, and perhaps a stub from one of your paychecks. Or, if you're self-employed, you may be asked for a copy of your most recent tax return.
- A completely filled out and signed contract, including a list of your most recent landlords, along with their telephone numbers. And, yes, they will be called.
- The name of your bank, and perhaps the account number as well. Some will even demand to see a bank statement. (This is unusual but not illegal.)

In your present circumstances, you may find it impossible to get around these demands. If such is the case, my advice is to give in on most of the points but *not on the Social Security number.* (Once the SSN is used to check your credit, you can be targeted in a heartbeat.) Dress well, be polite, use your passport for ID, and offer to pay several months in advance. Above all, prepare beforehand to explain the reason—perhaps fear of a stalker—why you are simply unable to allow anyone to have your Social Security number. If you must furnish a copy of your tax return, black out your Social Security number, and then (to make sure it cannot still be read in front of a strong light) make a copy of that copy.

Warning: If you succeed in renting an apartment without revealing your Social Security number, then never pay the rent with a personal check. Otherwise, a PI can trace it back to your bank and your bank *does* have your Social Security number. Instead, pay either in cash or with a money order purchased at a post office, a supermarket, or a convenience store.

If, at the present time, you see no way around acceding to all of the landlord's demands, do not despair. Get a short lease or rent month-by-month while you make your plans to move on to a more private location.

RENTING A HOUSE FROM ITS OWNER

If you choose to rent a house rather than apartment, you may be able to solve the Social Security number problem, especially if you have money available from an emergency fund. Watch the classified ads and especially Craigslist. Also, check with real estate agencies. The object is to deal directly with the owner of the property. The following is an example from a friend of ours that I'll refer to as John Martin Tallman.

John moved to a new area where he was having a home custom-built. Due to a myriad of delays and problems, the builders were six months away from completion. He checked the classifieds and found this one:

> For lease: 3,000 sq. ft. home on golf course.
> $1700/month plus $2000 deposit. Credit
> check mandatory. Call Amy at 783-99xx.

The "credit check mandatory" did not scare John. As "Martin" Tallman he called Amy for an appointment, showed up in a conservative suit and tie, introduced himself as an investor who was considering a move to the area, and asked to see the property. The house had been on the market for nearly a year. After six months, the asking price of $495,000 had been reduced to $449,000, but, due to a current recession, the home had still not sold. Amy's boss, who had built the home on speculation, had decided to lease it out until the market improved. Although the owner had hoped to lease it out for a minimum of one year, it was agreed that John could lease for just six months, with an option to extend the lease to one year.

"You mentioned a credit report in your ad," he said. "I prefer to keep my private affairs private, and for that reason I never give out my Social Security number. Since I always—"

"Sir, we need your Social Security number for a credit report."

"As I started to say, since I always pay cash, a file has never been opened for me in any credit agency."

"Nevertheless," said Amy, "we can make a routine check. If nothing turns up—"

"Excuse me," said John with a smile, holding up his hand. "If you send in a request, they will open a file for me, and there goes my privacy. Now then, I totally understand that you do not plan to lease this home unless you are sure that the monthly payments will come in, right?"

"Of course, and that's why—"

"In my case, no monthly payments will be involved. I'll pay cash in advance."

"For all six months?"

"Yes, for all six months, and if I extend the lease at the end of that time, I will again pay for six months. I can give you the name of my attorney in San Francisco who will confirm that I am a law-abiding citizen. Here is my passport (showing it), and I will leave you a photocopy. We have no children, we throw no parties, my wife's only hobby in life is scrubbing and cleaning, we have no pets, and neither of us smoke. You can leave the utilities in the present name and I'll leave a deposit with you to cover them. I can have a bank cashier's check for you within the hour. How shall I have it made out?"

"I'll have to talk to my boss."

"Fine, I'd like that. Is he here?"

"No, I'll have to call him. Could you come back at this same time tomorrow?" The lease went through the next day. Note:

- No one was called for a reference.
- No Social Security number was given.
- The lease was in John's middle and last name only, and did not include the name of his wife.
- He listed no previous addresses.
- Not one of the utilities was put into his name.
- He never received any mail or deliveries at that address.
- He avoided giving his date of birth.

Pay close attention to that last item. One problem with a passport is that it *does* list the date of birth, and the date of birth is sometimes used in databases in lieu of an SSN. John, however, was prepared in advance for that problem. He had previously photocopied his passport, eliminated the date of birth on the copy, and then copied it again. When he met with Amy the next day, he was ready.

"Here, again, is my passport," he said, showing it and then putting it back in his pocket. "And here is a photocopy for your files." The altered copy went into the files without a second glance.

At no time during the six months of the lease did John ever mention that he was having a home built in the area, and when he moved out he "neglected" to leave any forwarding address. (If you are thinking to yourself that very few persons can pay six months' rent in advance, please review the final question at the end of this chapter.)

TRAVEL TRAILERS AND MOBILE HOMES

No Social Security number is needed if you purchase a travel trailer or a mobile home for cash and register it in the name of a limited liability company. If you are determined to own your own home, I suggest buying an older mobile home in a park and then fixing it up while you live there. We have some Mexican friends who do this on a regular basis. They pay not more than $8,000, live in it for a year while fixing it up, and then sell it for up to $15,000.

REAL ESTATE PURCHASES AND SALES

A Social Security number is required for the IRS reporting forms, even if you do pay cash. Although I don't consider giving your Social Security number under this condition is high risk—the IRS has it anyway—you are not without options. One is to never actually *buy* real estate. Rent, lease, or take options. Or, you can purchase and sell in the name of a New Mexico limited liability company if you first obtain a tax identification number (TIN).

FALSE SOCIAL SECURITY NUMBERS

A federal court of appeals has ruled that using a false SSN to obtain a driver's license is illegal. Other than that, there appears to be no legal penalty for giving a wrong number as long as there is no intent to deceive a government agency, commit fraud, or obtain a specific benefit.

Nevertheless, *I do not recommend this.* What if the number you choose turns out to be that of a drug dealer, a child pornographer, or someone who died prior to the year you use it? The wisest course is to give your true number but only when absolutely required, or else no number at all.

OBTAINING CREDIT

In many cases it may be extremely difficult to obtain credit without revealing your Social Security number, so you'll have to ask yourself a question: *"How desperately do I need this credit?"* The correct answer should be, "Not *that* desperately!" In the *Computer Privacy Handbook*, author André Bacard quotes his grandfather's opinion of credit:

> *I'm 80 years old and free because I never owed a dime. Young people are addicted to credit. Mark my words, André. Credit will lead to a police state in America. I hope I die before then.*

My Scottish father and my Norwegian mother ran their lives the same way, quoting Proverbs 22:7 to my sister and me: "The borrower is a servant to the man doing the lending." The advice was sound. I pass it on to you.

RUN YOUR LIFE ON A CASH BASIS

If you truly wish to become invisible, never apply for personal credit. (There is occasionally a business exception but credit in this case should be extended only to your corporation or limited liability company.) We raised our children to pay cash or go without, we recommend the same to all our friends, and we stand by our own example even when discussing the International Dream of "Owning Your Own Home."

Incidentally, home ownership is overrated, as millions discovered when the values plummeted in the last few years. It is usually cheaper to rent or lease your living quarters. Further, should disaster strike from whatever direction, as a renter you can move before the sun rises tomorrow morning. The homeowner, on the other hand, will dawdle and procrastinate, and in some cases this delay can be fatal.

Until my wife and I were in our fifties, we *rented*, period. When we finally did build our first home on Lanzarote Island, perched on a cliff 1,500 feet above the Atlantic, we paid cash for every brick and block. Further, we were mentally prepared to walk away and leave this home if we had to. Since then we've built homes both there and in North America, always for cash, and only because we can afford this totally unnecessary luxury.

When the day comes that we can't afford to walk (or run) away and leave a house behind, we'll sell it, stash the cash, and go back to renting. In, as always, another name.

QUESTIONS & ANSWERS

Can I get by without a passport, and still maintain my privacy?

Yes of course . . . if you never travel by air, never pay in a store by check, never cash a check at a bank, never receive a registered letter, and are never otherwise called upon to prove your age or identity. Since this may not be practical for you, let's discuss another aspect of drivers' licenses.

A recent news program on national television discussed the sale of pictures that go with state drivers' licenses. The buyer is a company called Image Data. What had previously been kept secret was now made public (i.e., that the source of Image Data's financing came from the U.S. Secret Service). Image Data *says* the only use for these pictures will be for businesses that accept checks. They will scan your driver's license and check the picture on the screen to be sure it is really you. Two questions arise:

1. What use does the U.S. Secret Service have in mind for these pictures?
2. Why was Image Data attempting to hide the U.S. Secret Service connection?

I cannot answer these questions. What I can do, however, is to continue to urge you not to use your driver's license for anything other than showing it to a policeman if you are stopped for a violation. (And do all within your power never to be stopped!)

Remember, for the past thirty-five years, most states have been selling the data from driver's licenses. This includes your height, weight, and home address, none of which shows up on a passport. Also, if an investigator wishes to check you out, one of the places he will check is at the DMV in the state in which you live. I therefore say—once again—that one of the very best ways to maintain your privacy is to obtain a passport and use it alone for identification. (On the rare occasion when a second piece of ID is required, use something other than your driver's license.)

What if a Social Security number is required for a hunting or fishing license?

Many states do require a Social Security number for registering a boat or buying a hunting or fishing license. (The boat, of course, can be registered in the name of a limited liability company.) You may wish to hunt or fish in another state—one that does not require a Social Security number. The nonresident license will cost you more, but if saving money is your goal, you'll do better if you just obtain your meat and fish at the local super-market.

Can't I just apply for a new Social Security number?

Many books have been published with advice about how to illegally obtain a new Social Security number. Some authors recommend you tell some wild story about how you were living in the jungles of New Guinea and just got back. More often, it is suggested you comb old newspapers for children who died young, and obtain—or fake—their birth certificate. These books are out of date because the Social Security Administration now requires anyone eighteen or older to show up in person with original or certified documents to prove age, identity, and U.S. citizenship, along with positive proof that no card has ever been issued previously. There are just three exceptions. These are for:

1. Those relocated with new identities under the Federal Witness Security Program.

2. Individuals who can prove they were victims of "identity theft" when criminals used their number repeatedly to get credit cards, make loans, and engage in other financial transactions.

3. Abused women who are hiding from husbands, ex-husbands, or former lovers. Until the latter part of 1999, only about 150 new numbers were granted each year. Since then, however, the Social Security Administration has been granting new numbers much more freely. In addition to original documents establishing your age, identity, and U.S. citizenship or lawful alien status, you will be asked for both your old and new names if you have changed your name. You must also present evidence showing you have custody of children for whom you are requesting new numbers; and evidence you may have documenting the harassment or abuse. The best evidence of abuse will come from third parties such as police, medical facilities, or

doctors. Other evidence may include court restraining orders; letters from shelters, family members, friends; counselors or others who have knowledge of the domestic violence or abuse. (For additional information about new numbers for abused women, go to the agency's Web site, www.ssa.gov/pubs/10093.html.)

Can I avoid giving my Social Security number on the basis of Revelation, Chapter 13?

I assume you are referring to the belief, held sincerely by some, that a Social Security number is the "mark of the beast." It is true that in the past, several persons have won court cases objecting on religious grounds to state requirements for a SSN as a condition to receiving a driver's license. In *Leahy v. District of Columbia*, the circuit court upheld John C. Leahy's religious objection to providing his Social Security number in order to get a driver's license.

Later, five plaintiffs sued the city of Los Angeles on religious objection grounds, objecting to the state's requirement that driver's license applicants must provide a Social Security number as a condition to getting a license. They won the case in the State Superior Court, but I believe the state appealed that decision.

If you really, truly believe that the use of a Social Security number violates your religious beliefs, then take your stand. If you go to jail—and some have—you will be suffering for what you feel is a righteous cause. But if you are thinking of challenging the authorities and just using religion as an excuse, then I urge you to back off. Join the rest of us who do furnish the number when absolutely necessary . . . but never otherwise.

You cited an example of a friend who paid his rent six months in advance in order to avoid giving out his SSN. But

what if we can barely scrape together a deposit and one *month in advance?*

If you are that broke, set the privacy issues aside for the moment. Get right to work on setting up an emergency fund—$5,000 minimum. (If you are making monthly payments on nonessentials like furniture, TV, or a fancy car, *sell them*.) Until you reach your goal, pay for nothing other than rent, gasoline, minimal repairs on an old car, utilities, insurance, and groceries. No cable TV, no movies, no newspapers, no soft drinks, no eating out, no alcohol, no cigarettes, and no new clothes or shoes. Don't tell me it cannot be done. I know Mexicans with minimum-wage jobs who send money to their parents back in Mexico *every month*.

Once you have your emergency fund in place, you can then—when necessary—pay your rent for six months in advance. This is the same as money in the bank.

YOUR ALTERNATE NAMES AND SIGNATURES

Anyone can sign your name. If your attorney, CPA, or anyone else warns you that you cannot legally sign another person's name, ask them to prove it. The only caveats are that the person whose name you are about to sign would confirm that you are authorized to do so, and that this action is not remotely associated with fraud.

Example: You have the tax return for your Wyoming corporation, Oliver's Oddities, Inc., ready to mail on the due date. However, you forgot that your cousin Oliver, who is substituting for you as the sole director, will have to sign. And Oliver is currently on an Arctic fishing trip. As long as you are absolutely convinced that Oliver would have signed, if he were present, then go ahead and sign his name. All the IRS wants to see is *a* signature. My only suggestion here is that, when Oliver returns, have him sign an acknowledgment affirming for the private corporate records that permission was given to sign his name. Clip this to your copy of the return.

IF YOU *SAY* IT'S YOUR SIGNATURE,
THEN IT'S YOUR SIGNATURE

Example: Your husband John is off hunting elk in the Rocky Mountains when an unforeseen emergency leaves you short of cash for Saturday night bingo. In the morning's mail comes his Social Security check. Can you sign his name and deposit his check in your joint account?

Yes, because you know that, if any question comes up later, he will acknowledge your signature as his own. Naturally, you sign the check *before* you go to the bank. (*Note:* Many husbands and wives practice signing each other's signatures for just such purposes as this, and some are skilled enough to fool any banker in the land.)

> *Warning:* If, instead of going hunting, John ran off with Flossy Floozie from the office, he will *not* want you to sign his name, in which case, repeat after me:
> **"DO . . . NOT . . . SIGN!"**

YOU CAN USE ANY NUMBER OF DIFFERENT
SIGNATURES, INCLUDING ILLEGIBLE ONES

In fact, among European businessmen, illegible is the order of the day. I used to work with a banker in Santa Cruz de Tenerife. His name was Hector Adelfonso de la Torre Romero y Ortega. This was his signature:

"But why," I'm often asked, "would anyone want an illegible signature?" Well, for signing letters to your friends, you do not want one, but why not have an alternative, illegible signature you can reproduce at will? Here are two reasons why such signatures are used so widely in Europe:

- If a copy of a secret letter comes to light, the identity of the signer will not be evident.
- Bank accounts can be in the name of another person or in the name of a legal entity, and the one receiving such a check will have no clue as to the signer. (*Note*: There should be no problem, in any event, with the bank itself. Only a few of the smallest banks actually check signatures.)

AN ALTERNATE NAME

Why would you, a model citizen and taxpayer, ever temporarily need another name? The reasons given in many books include overwhelming debts, threatened vengeance by wrathful in-laws, a marriage gone bad, being listed on a criminal site, included on a no-fly list by mistake, or getting on a Mafia hit list. But circumstances and situations can change in a heartbeat, and thousands of persons living a tranquil life one day have resorted to flight the next.

The fact that you are right and the charges are wrong may be meaningless—just ask any lawyer if he can get you justice. The stock answer is, "How much justice can you *afford*?"

By the way, let's not call your second name an "alias," that's only for the criminal types. What you want is a perfectly respectable alternate name, an assumed name, a nom de plume, nom de guerre, also called a pseudonym. (These can be used almost anywhere, as long as there is no intent to defraud.)

Have you ever thought about being in the movies, even as an "extra"? Then you'll want a *stage name*. Or perhaps you'd like to be a writer, like Samuel Clemens, aka Mark Twain? If so, your journey will begin with the first step, choosing a *pen name*. Women often use their maiden names in business and either men or women can adopt the British custom of using a hyphenated name. Hillary Clinton, for example, could do this. She could use Hillary *Rodham-Clinton* and in an alphabetical listing such a name would be under "R." However, a pen name can be any name you like.

For privacy, nothing beats a common name because it is so hard to identify which one belongs to you. (Just ask any PI.) If your name is, for example, Meinhard Leuchtenmueller, you will want to use a much more common name where possible. Suppose you will be working out of an address in Minneapolis. Why not use something like M. Anderson for your mail-order business? (There are more than 10,000 M. Andersons in the United States, most of them in the upper Midwest.) Or, if you work out of Miami or Los Angeles, you might try M. Hernandez. Check the local telephone directories for the most common names in your area.

TITLES

A surprising number of people—even in America—have a desire for some sort of title that will make them feel important. If they wish, they can call themselves a doctor, a lawyer, a CPA, or a captain with Northwest Airlines. That is, in the United States. (Do not try this in Europe!) In the Land of the Free, it is not what you call yourself but what you practice. If you are not a "CPA," do not advise anyone on taxes. If you pose as a lawyer, do not give any opinions on the law. For many, the title of choice will be "doctor." The following are some guidelines for wannabe doctors:

DO NOT GIVE ADVICE

Explain that you are not "that kind" of a doctor. Maybe you deal only with viruses from Chad. Also, you will certainly be truthful when—if called upon for some emergency—you say you are not in "practice" and do not therefore carry malpractice insurance. Frank Abagnale Jr., in his intriguing book *Catch Me If You Can*, says that when passing himself off as a doctor in the state of Georgia, he had a standard answer for anyone who asked what kind of doctor he was.

"I'm not practicing right now," he said, identifying himself as a pediatrician. "My practice is in California and I've taken a leave of absence for one year to audit some research projects at Emory University and to make some investments."

However, Abagnale did not always stick to his standard answer. On one occasion, an attractive brunette mentioned an "odd, tight feeling" in her chest. He did examine her privately. His diagnosis was that her brassiere was too small.

Do not do as he did unless you are willing to risk both civil and criminal charges of assault.

IT IS PERMISSIBLE TO ACT THE PART

Subscribe to a couple of medical magazines and carry one around. Wear a smock with a stethoscope in the pocket.

"You can even join the county medical society" says Jack Luger, in his book *Counterfeit I.D. Made Easy*. He says you can simply explain that you are not licensed in the state because you're doing research rather than holding a practice and that the most that can happen is they'll refuse to accept you.

MEDICAL RECORDS

The following is from a long article in the *Los Angeles Times* under the headline "Some Fear Seeking Care":

> A survey commissioned by the California HealthCare Foundation . . . documents that one in six Americans engages in "privacy protected behaviors," such as paying out of pocket for care otherwise covered by insurance, lying to their doctor about their medical history or being afraid to get care. . . .
>
> LaTanya Sweeney, an assistant professor of public policy at Cannegie Mellon University in Pittsburgh, demonstrated how easy it is to pierce the privacy in so-called anonymous medical records. Even when names have been stripped off records that contain date of birth, sex, race, and diagnostics, she can readily re-identify the individual by cross-referencing with a $20 voter registration list . . .
>
> In one instance, she looked at data from the city of Cambridge, Mass., population 54,000, and was able to identify former Gov. William Weld because only five people in the city—and only one in his ZIP Code—had his date of birth.

The conclusions that some people may draw from articles like this are listed below, along with my comments in parentheses:

- Do not give the doctor a complete medical history. (If you are going to a doctor for some normal medical reason, why—*assuming it does not apply to the case at hand*—would you list any visit to a psychiatrist for depression, or admit to any history of a venereal disease?)

- Change your birth date and withhold your Social Security number. (If you are using your medical insurance or making a claim to Medicare you must, of course, list your true date of birth and SSN. If you pay cash, however, change your date of birth and withhold your Social Security number.)

- Get off voter rolls and never return. (Whether or not you do this must be a personal decision.)

WEB SITES ADVERTISING FAKE ID

If you google "fake ID" you will get millions of hits. Ignore them all. At one time I sent money orders to various sites, just to check them out. Sometimes I received a grossly inferior product. Other times I received nothing at all. Eventually I stopped losing time and money this way.

Lee Lapin, author of *How to Get Anything on Anybody—The Newsletter*, came to the same conclusion. In one of his issues he wrote, in capital letters, "AS OF THIS WRITING I KNOW OF NO, ZERO, SITES THAT SELL ANYTHING EVEN VAGUELY WORTH BUYING!"

QUESTIONS & ANSWERS

How can I change my name legally?

I seldom recommend you do this. After all, you may use one or more additional names and still retain your legal name. However, to answer the question: When you legally change your name, you *abandon* your present name and choose a new one of your liking.

Should you chose this route, I suggest you choose a common name, one that will be shared with thousands of others. In the United States, 25 percent of men of retirement age have one of the following names: John, William, James, Charles, or George. As for a last name, why not pick a family name from the *Mayflower*? Here are some of the more common names, culled from a complete list kept by Christopher Jones, Master, 1620:

Alden	Fuller	Turner
Browne	Martin	Warren
Carter	Priest	White
Clarke	Rogers	Williams
Cooke	Thompson	

The usual rules apply, i.e., the new name may not be the same as that of a famous person, nor can there be intent to defraud.

The use method   The use method requires no lawyer, no trip to the courthouse, and is not legally registered anywhere. Keep in mind, however, that you will not be able to open a bank account nor obtain a driver's license with the new name. However, if you pay cash, you may be able to get by with no problem. You will of course always use your true name in the following instances:

- When stopped by the police.
- For your auto and home insurance.
- For your income tax return.
- When traveling by ship, train, or air.

The court method   State statutes regarding legal name changes vary, so if you dislike the requirements in one state, check those in another. A lawyer is not necessary, so do not use one; they keep records in their files. Various books on name changes are available and you may find one or more of these at your local library. A date will be set for a court appearance and the judge will question you to make sure you are not changing your name for a deceitful purpose. If no such reason emerges, you can expect approval of your new name, and this name change will be valid in all fifty states and the District of Columbia. You will now be able to obtain a new driver's license and a new passport.

With this method, of course, you have left a paper trail. There is a file somewhere that contains the name you were born with.

> *Warning*: Some name-changers have been known to bribe an employee to take their old file and accidentally "misfile" it inside another, thicker file—some old case that's long since been settled. Although that does solve the "paper trail" problem, do not do it. It is a criminal action. Some doing this have been caught. Further, it is not necessary. I have already outlined ways to use alternate names in a 100 percent legal way. Reread this chapter again.

What do you think about fake passports?

In 1992 I was offered a passport from the "Dominion of Melchizedek." I turned it down. (As you may remember, Melchizedek was the King of Salem, mentioned in Genesis. No country was ever named for him.) Less than a year later, I read about one of the promoters being arrested at Incline Village, on the Nevada side of Lake Tahoe. What surprised me wasn't that he was arrested—I expected that—but that before being caught he'd sold *thousands* of the fake Melchizedek passports at inflated prices. Another "country" sometimes mentioned is the "Principality of Sealand." Before you fall for that one, google the words "Principality, Sealand, hoax."

I never recommend false passports, not even from former nations such as British Honduras (now Belize). All this does is draw attention to yourself, which you do not need.

How do private investigators track down celebrities to serve subpoenas?

First, they track down the name they were born with. Next, they discover the true date of birth. Once they have that combination, they investigate property purchases, marriages, family members, churches, charities, clubs, lawsuits, pets, memberships, schools, and vehicles.

The PIs who have a 100 percent success rate in doing this are the ones that have unlimited backing. Offer one of these specialists enough money, and they will track down any celebrity, anywhere on earth. They could also track *you* down, as I said earlier in this book, but unless you've made some mortal enemies who have the necessary funds and are willing to spend them, don't lose any sleep over the prospect.

LANDLINE TELEPHONES AND ANSWERING MACHINES

In 1977, California millionaire Gary Allen Bandy purchased land near the rural community of Gardiner on Washington State's Olympic Peninsula. He then proceeded to build a castle and other medieval buildings, bringing in artists to carve intricate Norwegian trolls on wooden posts. He was subsequently featured in the *National Enquirer* as an eccentric millionaire surrounded by his medieval buildings and trolls.

In 1991, a son was born to Gary and his wife, Eva. Later, they separated, and in 1995, divorce proceedings were begun. Eva hired attorney Natalie De Maar. Gary hired attorney Steven Fields. Bitter charges flew back and forth as Gary and Eva battled for custody of son Geoff, now four.

Eva Bandy rented a home in the upscale community of Gig Harbor, at the northern end of the Tacoma Narrows Bridge. The owner lived just across the street. His name was James Wilburn, and he was a private investigator. What followed next was the subject of an article in the *Peninsula Daily News*:

Bandy's attorney, Steven Fields, was leaving a voice-mail message for Eva Bandy's attorney, Natalie De Maar. He was using the speakerphone. Sitting in his office was Bandy and another attorney. Fields thought he disconnected the speakerphone and proceeded to have a conversation with Bandy.

What Fields failed to realize was that the speakerphone was not disconnected. Therefore, when Bandy admitted that he had hired an investigator to put a wiretap on his wife's phone, his words were being recorded on attorney Natalie De Maar's answering-machine tape. The tape eventually wound up in the hands of the FBI, who then raided Bandy's home at Gardiner Beach and his fifty-foot yacht at a nearby marina. A week later, Bandy was arrested while on a trip through Idaho.

What have we learned so far?

1. Some PIs will bug cars and residences if the pay is right.
2. Some lawyers cannot be trusted with confidential information.
3. When it comes to speakerphones (to paraphrase Murphy's law), any mistake that can be made will be made, and at the worst possible moment.

We can learn more. Because he ordered an illegal wiretap. Gary Allen Bandy was sentenced to two months in prison and five years of probation. He was also fined $21,138.

Attorney Steven Fields did not go to jail. There are no laws against stupidity.

The private investigator did not go to jail. The article did not say if he turned state's evidence, so I can only state a general truth: No matter how much you trust an attorney, a doctor, a CPA, or a private investigator, when a prosecutor starts talking jail time, these and other professionals will give you up in a heartbeat. (The G. Gordon Liddy types are a disappearing species.)

TELEPHONE SECURITY

"Telephone security" is an oxymoron because a telephone conversation is never secure. The calls go over hard lines, may be beamed up and down from satellites, or travel via digital or analog radio waves, and they can be intercepted.

If you have any deep dark secrets to tell, and *if you suspect you may be under surveillance*, it's best to just write a letter and mail it inside a post office.

UNLISTED NUMBERS

An unlisted number is no longer the protection it used to be. Many unlisted telephone numbers are now available on the Internet (often requiring a small fee), and reverse searches are available as well.

Example: You obtain an unlisted landline with call blocking. Nevertheless, you one day need to call some company and all they list is a toll-free number. *All* such numbers (800, 888, 877, and 866) have Automatic Number Identification (ANI) and once you call them, your unlisted number is captured. Eventually your number will be in various databases available to private investigators. It may even show up on databases available to the general public.

Further, many Level Three PIs have contacts inside both cell and landline companies who can run a search by either a name, or an address. Once your number is obtained, that can lead to your street address. Therefore, use extreme caution before giving out your home telephone number. Instead (as outlined in chapter 11), use a pager number or a prepaid cell phone number to the general public.

HOW TO LIST YOUR NAME

Given that—despite having an unlisted telephone number—the name you give the telephone company may show up on a national database, do your best to disguise it. Try one of the following:

- Wife's middle name and maiden name.
- Your middle name or initial, and last name.
- The name of a friend or relative (find someone with a very common name) who is willing to have the phone put in their middle/last or middle/maiden names.

Another system that many have used successfully is to explain that you are a writer and that your telephone number must be listed in your well-known *pen* name. (In this case, you may choose to have the name listed.) The usual procedure is that you will be instructed to go to one of the company's offices and prove your true identity, so they have that for their files. They will then allow you to list whatever name you've chosen. The trick here is to choose the most common name you can think of, with no middle initial, so that the name will be lost in a sea of similar names.

I am partial to first names like John, Robert, Mary, and Elizabeth, with surnames such as Johnson, Cohen, McDonald, Anderson, Rodriguez, and Brown. If moving to a new area, I'd first spend an hour or two with the local telephone directory—checking for the most common names in that area. Many will be identical, which is of course what you want.

HOW NOT TO ANSWER THE TELEPHONE

Let's say your names are Lawrence and Jennifer Barrington but your telephone is in the name of Jennifer's middle name plus her maiden name, i.e., Suzanne Martin. Until the present moment, you or members of your family may have been answering the telephone with phrases such as:

"Larry Barrington here."
"Barrington residence."
"Hi, this is Jenny!"

However, what if the telephone company is calling? Remember, the name *they* have for this residence is Suzanne Martin. Or, it could be a private detective on the line, or a process server with a subpoena in his pocket. Therefore, a simple "Hello" or "Good morning" will suffice. Let the *caller* be the one to mention a name, and when necessary, answer with a question. For example:

Caller A: Good morning! How are you today, sir?

You: What are you selling? (When "How are you?" rather than your name, follows "Hello," you know it's a salesperson.)

Caller B: Ms. Suzanne Martin?

You: What is this in reference to, please?

Caller B: This is Cora with the Crystal County Sheriff's Department. (Not to panic. Don't speak; *wait for more information.*)

Caller B: We're sponsoring the Crystal County Crusade Against Crime, and for a small donation you can—

You: Suzanne won't be back from Italy for at least two months, but thank you for calling, good-bye.

Practice beforehand, and in time you'll stop getting sweaty hands and an accelerated heartbeat.

CHANGING YOUR LISTING

If you are not yet willing or able to move to a new location, you may still contact the telephone company to say you are moving away. (If asked, tell them you are moving to Mexico City or to London. Set a date for the service to be discontinued.)

A few days or weeks later, order a new telephone, which will of course have a different number. If you are using someone else to do this for you, have him or her make the call. This person will *not* admit to having had service before, nor will a SSN be given.

Since no credit history is available, the telephone company will ask for a cash deposit to ensure payment. Stop by their offices or mail in a money order for the requested amount—usually a few hundred dollars. Assuming you pay your bills on time, expect your deposit to be returned to you at the end of one year.

CORDLESS PHONES

Despite the booming market in cell phones, not everyone is getting rid of their landline phones—many if not most of which are cordless. The sound quality is still better than any cell phone, and the new models are better than ever, thanks to 1.9 GHz DECT (Digital Enhanced Cordless Telecommunications). Some models support Bluetooth technology. This means you can route cell calls through your cordless phone, giving you better reception in otherwise hard-to-reach places.

Nevertheless, technology advances too quickly to endorse any kind of normal telephone. The below is from theregister.co.uk:

> Cryptographers have broken the proprietary encryption used to prevent eavesdropping on more than 800 million cordless phones worldwide, demonstrating once again the risks of relying on obscure technologies to remain secure. The attack is the first to

crack the cipher at the heart of the DECT, or Digital Enhanced Cordless Telecommunications, which encrypts radio signals as they travel between cordless phones in homes and businesses and corresponding base stations.

For one possible exception, see the first question at the end of this chapter.

THE TELEPHONE AT THE OTHER END

When you make a sensitive call, make sure the person at the other end is on a secure line. A few years ago, I called an older woman who at that time lived in a large trailer court on one of the islands in Puget Sound, Washington. As the conversation grew more serious, she said, "Just a minute, Jack, I'm going to switch to a more secure telephone on a second line."

Oh-oh! When she came back on the line, I learned she had an old, cheap cordless phone. And even more troubling, she then told me she *knew* her calls were being monitored. She said there were some "militia types" in the trailer court, and that some of the neighbors had made comments about conversations she'd had on the portable phone!

A really serious problem arises when you call someone whose telephone—unknown to them—is tapped. In that case, no matter what preventive measures have been taken, your home number will be revealed. If, therefore, you are wary that the person you are calling may be under surveillance, go to the extra trouble of communicating in some other way.

"HACKER-PROOF" ANSWERING MACHINES

There is no such thing as a hacker-proof answering machine. If I were an electronics engineer, that would be my first project—to invent a secure answering machine. One PI I know, who employs six agents, says this is at the top of his wishlist—a number where his agents could call in to leave and pick up messages in absolute secrecy.

As this is written, there is an ongoing controversy involving the *News of the World* and other British tabloid newspapers published by News International, a subsidiary of News Corporation. It appears that employees of the newspaper have been engaged in phone hacking, police bribery, and exercising improper influence in the pursuit of publishing stories, especially in regards to celebrities, politicians, and members of the British Royal Family. The FBI is now investigating complaints that they may have been accessing voice mails of some Americans *as far back as September 2001.*

Currently, a Level Three PI can not only check the messages on your answering machine, he can record them and then delete them before you even have a chance to listen to them. Think about that one, eh?

CALLS TO 911

When you call 911, your true address shows up on the operator's monitor, along with whatever name your telephone service is under. If it is listed in another name, will you be able to give a reason for this when the police arrive? (Even if the call was for an ambulance, the police usually arrive first.) To illustrate both the problem and the solution, consider the experience we once had in a western state.

I was sitting at my computer, working on the 2004 version of this book, when I happened to glance out the window. Here came Walter, one of my neighbors at that time, dragging his big black dog on a leash, racing up to my door. He started pounding on it before I could get there to open.

"A horse just fell on Julie," he exclaimed, pointing to the east pasture, "and she broke her leg! *Call 911!*"

Thoughts raced through my aging brain: *If I call 911 on the landline, my call blocking will not work.* Our phone was in another name. I would be asked for my name, and it would be compared with the readout on the computer screen. While I stood at the door, hesitating not more than two seconds, Walter spread his hands out and shouted, *"JACK, CALL 911!"*

Better, I decided, to use my cell phone. I dashed back into the house, grabbed my cell phone out of its charging unit, and called 911.

This is 911 said a female voice, adding the name of the county.

I'm calling from a cell phone and—

Yes, I know. What is the emergency?

A lady just had an accident with her horse and broke her leg.

Where is the location? (I described the general location of the pasture.)

How old is this lady?

I don't know, maybe fifty or sixty.

Where are you now? (I named the road and said I would wait there to direct the emergency vehicle.)

What is your name and where do you live?

One moment please, something has just—(At this point I punched the power off on my cell phone.)

I went to the street and was there to direct the emergency vehicle in on the proper lane. A neighbor was already on the scene with a blanket, so I evaporated before any of the crew could ask me if I was the one who called.

In chapter 5, I discussed the case of a Miami police detective's wife who called 911 and thus revealed their true address. They then had to sell their home and move. But did she have any options? I think she did, and you would do well to review these alternatives with other members of your family.

1. If she had a cell phone (and she should have!), she could have used that to make the call to 911.

2. Had prior arrangements been set up, she could have called a friend who would in turn call 911 from *her* home, directing the ambulance to such-and-such an address where the detective's wife was *visiting*.

3. When checking in at the hospital, she could have given their ghost address, adding that she was just housesitting for a friend when the emergency came up.

WATCH OUT FOR THIS SNEAKY TRICK

Suppose a private investigator wants to hear you talking to your lawyer (or mistress, or whomever). He may place a conference call, recording every word. Here is how it works. The first call would go to you, and when you answer, the PI punches HOLD and then speed-dials your lawyer. You start saying, "Hello? Hello?" Then your lawyer comes on the line. He recognizes your voice. Each of you may then *assume* the other person placed the call, and start to chat!

Remedy: When a call comes in from a sensitive party, and there is some confusion about who called whom, *ask*. If neither called the other, you have just had a heads up that someone is after one or both of you.

QUESTIONS & ANSWERS

In the case of a life-or-death situation where neither privacy nor legality matter, what is the fastest way to get help?

Call either the fire department or 911 and report a fire in progress. Captain Robert L. Snow, in his book *Protecting Your Life, Home, and Property*, says that if you live in a high-crime area and call 911 on a hot summer weekend and/or a busy day, there may be a delay in getting a policeman to your home. He says there have been cases where police dispatchers have listened as a caller was murdered before the police arrived.

Some persons, under these circumstances, have called the fire department and reported a fire. "This should be done only in desperate situations," says Snow, "since there will likely be some legal consequences later because of calling in a false fire alarm. . . . But if you have absolutely no doubt there is an intruder who knows you're in the home and is trying to get in anyway, there's a very good chance you will be raped, beaten, and/or murdered. At a time like this you can't really worry about legal niceties. There's not much point in being completely law-abiding if you're dead."

Sometimes I hear clicking noises on my telephone. I brought in a detective to check for bugs and he said there weren't any, but what if he was wrong? How can I be sure my telephone isn't tapped?

If the government is after you, they will do the tap at a central office, and no detective will ever track that one down. In fact, a little test might be to have Detective A install the best tap he knows, and then see if Detective B can find it. (Let me know if you do that; I've got $20 that says Detective B will miss it.) Here is the best advice you'll ever get about telephone security. Create a little label that says, THIS LINE IS TAPPED and stick it on every telephone.

Can international telephone calls be monitored without a warrant?

Of course, if they are beamed by microwave transmission. The National Security Agency (NSA) does this all the time. No warrant is needed to monitor microwave transmissions.

If I have Caller ID, will it always show the true number of an incoming call?

No. Even back in 1999, Mickey Hawkins, head of the FBI office in Tulsa, Oklahoma, in an interview for an article in the *Los Angeles Times*, said "We use a device that gives a different number."

Since then, any PI can spoof a number, and many average citizens have programs that do that, as well.

What is a "trap line"?

A *trap line* is a toll-free number used by private investigators to identify the location you are calling from. As soon as the target makes a call, the company providing this service contacts the PI to report the number and location of the incoming call. Remember, since the trap-line number starts with a toll-free area code (800, 888, 877, 866, or 855), you cannot block the transmission of information.

If you are the target, and the PI has only your ghost address, he may send you a convincing postcard or letter, asking you to either call him or send a fax. If you call or fax from home, he's got you.

Or, perhaps he does not have an address for you but he does have a telephone number of a friend or relative. He will call them while they are away at work, hoping for an answering machine. If there is one, he will leave a message—have so-and-so call me before tomorrow midnight! *"Urgent, there is a deadline, can't wait!"*

11

SMARTPHONES, DUMBPHONES, PAGERS

I just flew from Vancouver, British Columbia, to New York; took Delta from JFK to Madrid, and then Iberia 1,000 miles south to the Canary Islands. What a difference it makes when you travel with a smartphone! On the way to the airport, I could rebook or cancel my flight, view and change seat assignments, and access real-time standby and upgrade lists. Once I checked in online, a barcode could be e-mailed to my phone—the code to be scanned at security checkpoints and gates instead of a boarding pass. Once underway, I could track my checked luggage—including real-time carousel information—and also follow the status of claims on any delayed bags.

But I didn't do any of those things because my only mobile phone is a dumbphone, and I do not take it with me when I cross the pond. (I never check luggage, either.)

HOW THE CONTENTS OF YOUR CELL PHONE
MAY BE REVEALED

Some traffic cops in Michigan now carry Cellebrite cell phone extraction devices. They can access all the information on your cell phone within a few short minutes, and *it doesn't matter what you erased or when you erased it.*

IF ARRESTED, YOUR IPHONE, BLACKBERRY, OR ANDROID SMARTPHONE WILL BE SEARCHED

No search warrant required! At least that's the current situation in California (thanks to Governor Moonbeam), and it'll probably soon be the case in a state near you. Even dumbphones typically have information stored in text messages, voice mails, and call records. Thus, it is entirely possible that you can be brought into custody on *one* charge and end up being charged with something *else*, all because the police were able to search your phone without a warrant. So be careful what you keep on it!

CROSSING A BORDER?

Not only can baggage, laptops, and flash drives be searched, but whatever type of phone you carry can be searched as well. Make sure you never have any nude pictures of your young children in there, *especially* not if you enter Canada or the UK.

TRYING TO HIDE YOUR HOME ADDRESS FROM A LEVEL TWO OR LEVEL THREE PI?

He'll have your service provider ping your smartphone late at night. It will reveal your location, turned off or not, as long as the battery is in it. But suppose you remove the battery? If you need to make a call from home, you'll have to put the battery back in, no?

Ping!

YOUR VOICE-MAIL BOXES CAN BE HACKED

As far back as the year 2007, Clive Goodman, former *News of the World* royal correspondent, went to jail briefly for intercepting voice-mail messages of members of the British Royal family. Not much has changed—we are still at risk to determined snoops. For example, AT&T, Sprint, and T-Mobile do not require cell phone customers to use a password on their voice-mail boxes. Because of that, many people simply do not bother to make one up. Big mistake, and here's why. Any decent PI can use a spoofing program to make it appear he is calling from your number.

Further, with just a bit of additional personal information about you, he can gain access to the automated phone systems for Bank of America and Chase credit card holders. If, then, you have a BofA account or a credit card with Chase, he can come up with debts, late payments, and credit limits. Bank of America's computer will even read off a list of dozens of recent charges, including names of doctors and other businesses you may have patronized.

Even *with* passwords, some Level Three PIs may be able to get your messages, but using a password will usually protect you against the lower levels.

THINK YOU CAN HIDE FROM YOUR INTIMATE PARTNER?

Not necessarily, according to a poll taken by *Reader's Digest* in a November 2011 article titled "Do You Snoop?" But don't be too sure. The worst countries for partners who snoop were Brazil,

India, and the Russian Federation, and the least worst were China, France, and Australia, but in all nations there proved to be snoopers—especially between ages sixteen to forty-five. To quote just one of the many comments in the article:

> "I always check my boyfriend's cell phone when he's in the shower," says Faviana Andrade, 32, from São Paulo, Brazil. "I want to know who he's spending time with."

IDENTITIES CAN BE REVEALED VIA FACIAL RECOGNITION AND FACEBOOK

A study led by Alessandro Acquisti from Carnegie Mellon University combined the use of cloud computing, facial recognition, and public information from Facebook and other social networking sites. *Results:* Acquisti and his team identified college students walking on campus based solely on their face and information gathered online.

- They came up with the real names of members of an online dating site who'd used false names.
- The team then developed a smartphone application which gathers both online and offline information and displays it over the person's facial image on the phone.

SMARTPHONES ARE MORE VULNERABLE THAN PREVIOUSLY THOUGHT

High Tech Computer (HTC) Corporation is a Taiwan-based designer and manufacturer of smartphone devices. They create a base design and then offer their product to be sold rebranded by other companies, such as i-mate, or networks, such as T-Mobile or Orange. They also offer devices under their own HTC brand.

One of the posts on the Android Police Web site on October 5, 2011, was by Artem Russakovskii, headlined:

Massive Vulnerability In HTC Android Devices (EVO 3G, 4G, Thunderbolt, Others) Exposes Phone Numbers, GPS, SMS, Email Addresses, Much More

The following is just a brief quote from a long and scary article, pointing out how apps can open up information from almost any source.

> HTC also included another app called HtcLoggers.apk. This app is capable of collecting all kinds of data . . . and then [providing] it to anyone who asks for it by opening a local port. Yup, not just HTC, but anyone who connects to it, which happens to be any app with the INTERNET permission. Ironically, because a given app has the INTERNET permission, it can also send all the data off to a remote server. . . . In fact, HtcLogger has a whole interface which accepts a variety of commands . . . and no login/password are required to access said interface.

If you *must* have a smartphone, then to preserve your privacy have a nominee buy it and maintain it with his or her own credit or debit card. Even then, however, certain precautions must be observed. (I may have additional details on smartphone privacy available by the time you read this. Visit www.howtobeinvisible .com for more information.)

LIFE WITHOUT A SMARTPHONE

For many years I've used one of the mainstream cell-phone providers. I gave them a bank cashier's check for a $1,000 security deposit (in lieu of a Social Security number), my middle and last name, and they handed me a new phone on the spot. A year later, my deposit was returned to me.

The bills go to a remote address and are paid from there. It is never turned on except when I am away from home and expecting a call, or when I need to make one. Therefore it is rather difficult to locate the phone, should anyone try to do so. The service does include password-protected voice mail, which I usually check once a day.

The way one of my readers obtains his cell phones is to search for them on eBay or Craigslist. He says, "If you want a fairly private cell phone, buy a used Verizon cell and activate it on the Page Plus Cellular system. Been doing this for years."

PREPAID CELL PHONES

Although the per-minute cost is high, if you carry a cell phone only for the occasional emergency, a prepaid cell phone may be your best choice. You choose how many minutes you want, and how much money you want to spend. Advantages:

- No deposit.
- No contract.
- No credit check.
- No minimum monthly fee.
- No identification required.
- No request for a Social Security number.

Some are even disposable. You'll find them at stores such as Walmart and RadioShack, as well as at many places on the Internet. I suggest you first go to Amazon.com, click on "Electronics," search for "prepaid cell," and study the reader comments for each phone on the list.

USE A PAGER WITH YOUR CELL PHONE

Although clerks in electronics stores may tell you, "People don't use pagers anymore," pay no attention to them. I am a great fan of those small, cheap pagers that cost less than $10 a month. A big plus is that—unlike cell phones—*the basic models cannot be tracked.* A cell phone, which both receives and transmits, is tied to a single tower. As you move down the highway with the cell phone on (even though not in use), it transfers your number from tower to tower. With pagers, although they, too, use towers, there is a vital difference: Each tower broadcasts *all* the messages, and there is no clue as to which tower is used when your pager rings.

For example, suppose a friend is trying to locate you at a huge airport. A message goes out on all the loudspeakers: "Miss Loretta Lindstrom, please meet your party at gate 10 on the B concourse." Unless you decide to show up (only to discover a stalker, a PI, or the police), no one can possibly know you were even in the airport, much less in which part. The small, cheap pagers offer you this same protection.

The best way to use your pager is in conjunction with a cell phone that is not turned on. If you receive a message that appears urgent, either turn your cell phone on just long enough to reply, or go to a pay phone. Here is a simple code used by one of my readers. He carries a pager clipped to his belt and keeps his cell phone in his car. The pager is always on, and the cell phone is always off unless in use.

First digit: Is always 1, 2, or 3:

1. Call me in the next day or two.
2. Call back as soon as convenient.
3. Emergency!

Second digit: Will be between 1 and 7:

1. Call wife at home.
2. Call wife on cell phone.
3. Call wife at work.
4. Call secretary.
5. Call parents.
6. Call friends Larry and Carol.
7. Package received at ghost address.

Look how simple it is to translate these two-digit codes:

22. Call wife's cell phone number as soon as convenient.
15. Call parents, perhaps this evening.
31. Call home this very minute!

How often have you been asked for your telephone number, and have been reluctant to give it out? (One such example is when you're arranging a blind date.) From now on, *give out your pager number.* Take the time to record a greeting in your own words, such as: "This is Hillary. Please leave a message." (You will, of course, check for messages from time to time.)

QUESTIONS & ANSWERS

I'm in the UK and there are certain times when I must *make a confidential call. That being the case, what is the least-worst phone I should buy?*

Check out the GSMK CryptoPhones from Germany. These have the strongest encryption algorithms on the market and are the only secure phones I know of that come with full source code available for independent review. They are not in general use because they cost thousands of dollars but if you really need it, it may be money well spent.

What is the dumbest dumbphone I can get?

According to Engadget, it's John's Phone. According to a review:

> It certainly is basic. In the age of smartphones and cheap fea-turephones, John's Phone is more clearly defined by what it lacks than what it has: no fancy color touchscreen display; no camera; no 3G radio, WiFi, Bluetooth or even GPRS data; no FM radio; no user-accessible storage; and no music player or apps of any kind. It can't even send a text message. It's just a quad-band GSM phone with an ink pen and paper notepad tucked neatly into its capacious recesses. That's right, pen and paper.

What do you think about Zfone?

I've never used it, but I asked a PI friend to check it out. He an-swers, "Other than the GSMK CryptoPhone, Zfone is the only encryption system I'd trust for telephony."

Note: Zfone doesn't work with Skype. However, it does work well with services like MagicJack.

When I leave my car at the dealer's for servicing, shouldn't I give them my cell phone number and then leave it on, so I'll know when my car is ready?

If you carry a small pager, just give them that number and tell them to enter some simple number several times (such as 1111 or 7777) after the beep. This works equally well when you're waiting to pick up eyeglasses at the mall, at the golf course when your tee time is ready, or when your wife is ready to be picked up after the baby shower.

Do you recommend satellite telephones?

You'll see these advertised in *Power & Motoryacht* and other yachting magazines. They were developed for oceangoing ships, but some airlines use them now for passengers, and you and I can use them anywhere, even in an isolated mountain valley or while crossing the Sahara. At one time it appeared that communications via satellite were reasonably safe. However, as we later learned, the late Osama bin Laden—who used one in Afghanistan—had his calls monitored on a regular basis. Also, the minutes are unusually expensive. I seldom recommend them unless you have an oceangoing yacht or plan a trek to the South Pole.

Why don't you allow consultations by telephone?

This is one of the main reasons why I require my consulting clients to meet with me face-to-face. Intelligence agencies, as well as many divisions within law enforcement, have it drilled into their heads to never use the telephone if a face-to-face meeting is at all possible. "Never," they're told, "say *anything* over the phone you wouldn't wish to see in tomorrow's *New York Times*."

12

E-MAIL AND THE INTERNET

There is no fog so dense, no night so dark, no gale so strong as that found at Oregon's Columbia River bar, where more than 2,000 ships have been lost. As the great river meets the ocean, its mighty current collides with ocean swells, earning this patch of water the nickname, "Graveyard of the Pacific." When a river pilot boards a ship coming in from the Pacific, with the fog rolling and the waves building up, his CYA advice to the captain is:

"I suggest you drop the anchor until conditions improve."

Like the river pilot at the bar, my advice to you is, "I suggest you not use e-mail or the Internet until security increases." The ship captains usually ignore the pilot's advice, and you will probably ignore mine. Nevertheless, if or when disaster strikes you from cyberspace, remember: *You've been warned!*

THE STORY OF PAUL PETERS

MOSMAN NSW, AUSTRALIA. Paul Douglas Peters, a fifty-year-old Australian investment banker, entered the residence of William Pulver, a wealthy CEO in Sydney, Australia. Pulver's eighteen-year-old daughter Madeleine was home alone. Peters attached a bomb-like device to her neck and warned that it would go off if she moved. He then left a ransom note on a USB digital storage device looped around Madeline's neck. The note included instructions to e-mail him at dirkstraun1840@gmail.com.

Police searched Peters's USB device and came up with a name. They also obtained access to his e-mail. He checked his Gmail account three times on that afternoon—first from a library, then twice more from a video store. Surveillance cameras from both places recorded a man matching Peters's description around that time. In one picture his Range Rover was shown, including the license plate number. The vehicle was registered in Peters's name.

Peters then took a one-way flight from Sydney to Chicago and flew to Kentucky the next day, where—thanks to his e-mail trail—he was arrested in a joint operation between FBI agents and the NSW police. We can all be happy the man was caught, but we can also extract a few lessons:

IF YOU ARE EVER FORCED TO RUN, FOR ANY REASON

- Never write a secret message using Microsoft Word. The USB drive revealed the ransom note written in Word. It contained metadata about the document's author, including the name "Paul P."
- Never use e-mail for a secret message. Each time Peters accessed his account, his location became known.
- Never use a library or a video store to check your e-mail. When Peters did just that, video cameras caught both him and his Range Rover.
- Never use a vehicle registered in your own name.

EVEN A STRONG PASSWORD MAY NOT PROTECT YOU

In the fall of 2011, FBI agents arrested Christopher Chaney, thirty-five, on charges of hacking e-mail accounts of dozens of celebrities, including Scarlett Johansson, Mila Kunis, Christina Aguilera, and Renee Olstead. How did he do it?

It turned out to be the same method used in 2008 by David Kernell, when he obtained access to Sarah Palin's account by looking up biographical details such as her high school and birth date, then using Yahoo!'s account recovery for forgotten passwords. It seems that Chaney used publicly available sources to find information about the celebrities and used that information to gain access to their Yahoo!, Apple, and Google e-mail accounts.

LESSONS LEARNED

1. If a hacker wishes to get into your e-mail account, your password will not matter to him, he will plan to get around it.
2. First, he will search the Internet for any scrap of information about you.
3. Then he will access your account up to the point of password entry, where he'll click on "Forgot your password?"
4. Using information he's previously gathered about you, he'll go to work by guessing the answers. It may take hours, it may take days, and in some cases it may takes weeks, but that is how Chaney hacked into the e-mail accounts of more than fifty celebrities.

HOW TO PROTECT YOURSELF

If you are allowed to choose your own question, do so, and make it a tough one. Otherwise, use false information (and keep track of it somewhere safe). Were you born in Bemidji, Minnesota? List "Seville, Spain." Born 1/4/1970? List "4/1/1979". If the name of your first dog was Spot, list "SwissCheese," and so on.

E-MAIL IS NEVER SECURE

An e-mail message may linger on backup hard drives for years on end, and then come back to haunt you. (They are increasingly being used in civil and criminal cases.) Teach your children that a silly or profane e-mail in their youth could come back to bite them many years down the line.

Far too many people leave sensitive information sitting in their inbox—a treasure trove for criminals. And unfortunately, sometimes you do have to deal with sensitive information. Maybe you're submitting a school or job application. Perhaps a friend sent you something confidential. How do you protect these messages?

One option is to use a relatively secure e-mail service, the first feature of which is SSL, or Secure Socket Layers. You can tell a secure site by the first part of its Web address—it starts with "https." (The "s" at the end stands for "secure.") This is advertised to create an encrypted pathway between your computer and the e-mail provider's server. It makes it nearly impossible for hackers to steal messages en route. (I should note that https is available in Gmail and Hotmail but it isn't necessarily turned on by default.) All online banking services and all payment pages where you enter credit card numbers should start with https.

Another important feature is message encryption. E-mail is typically sent as plain text. If hackers intercept the e-mail, they can read it with no problems. Encrypted e-mail is much harder for hackers to read. In most cases, they won't be able to decrypt it. Encryption is best when both parties are on the same service.

The e-mail you send back and forth stays encrypted the whole way. It is also encrypted on the mail provider's servers. Even if hackers broke in, the message wouldn't be readable.

What if you're sending confidential information to a friend on another service? Some services let you password-protect the e-mail. Only a recipient with the password can open it. That adds another layer of protection against hackers. Of course, secure e-mail only takes you so far. There are other security aspects you need to consider. Here are three of the more important ones.

1. Make sure you have a strong unique password guarding your account. Include upper and lower case letters, a number, and at least one symbol. Otherwise, fancy encryption may be useless.

2. Use extreme care to avoid spyware and keyloggers. These can steal your passwords and send them to hackers, giving them full access to your accounts.

3. What about the recipients? You might send an encrypted message to a friend, but he or she could store it as plain text. If so, all a hacker needs to do is just to break into your friend's account.

"THIS MESSAGE WILL SELF-DESTRUCT" (TMWSD)

TMWSD is a secure, auto-deleted messaging service. They encrypt your message before they store it. Then, the first time the message is retrieved, they delete the encrypted content. Then, if you wish, you can even add a password. Rather than store your password, they hash it using a heavy-duty hashing utility (*bcrypt*), and then salt the encryption key with it for even more security.

This means that without the password no one other than you and the recipient can decrypt your secret message, not even them.

Go to ***www.thismessagewillselfdestruct.com*** and try it out right now.

YOUR INTERNET SERVICE PROVIDER

The moment you sign up for an Internet account, your invisibility begins to fade. At the government's request, every Internet service provider (ISP) must furnish—with no advance notice to you—the following information about your account:

- The name you gave them, and the address where bills are sent.
- Records of your Internet sessions (including session times and duration).
- Your telephone number or other subscriber account identifying number(s); including any Internet or network addresses assigned to you.
- The source of your payments, including any credit card or bank account numbers.
- The content of and other records relating to your electronic mail messages, including attachments.

Can you get by with a false name, a PO box address, and pay the bills by money order? Yes . . . but if the government ever decides to go after you, the ISP will be forced to give up the source of your connections—a source that may lead straight to your office or home.

INTERNET DANGERS

As one writer of a well-known magazine wrote:

> Web pages contain both excellent information and utter garbage,
> and it's up to us to sort it all out. We now face temptations that
> were unthinkable in times past—addictions to online gambling,
> to pornography, to finding love in all the wrong places, and an
> addiction to the Internet itself. Use of the Internet has resulted
> in runaway children, tragic marital problems, broken homes and
> ruined lives.

Sadly, my wife and I have seen the bitter consequences of
looking for "love in all the wrong places." For the two families
involved, it would have been infinitely better had they never had
access to the Internet.

Do I use the Internet? Yes, in this business I must, but make
no mistake—*you can live without the Internet.* Even with it, never
forget that the Internet is a mysterious and highly dangerous
place, seething with false information, viruses, worms, trojans,
spybots, spyware, hijackers, phishers, pornography traps, botnets,
and scams.

INTERNET SCAMS

New Internet extortion techniques arise on a daily basis. Here is
a typical example, this one aimed at those of you who use a computer at your place of employment.

1. You receive an unsolicited e-mail containing a link to a
   seemingly innocuous site such as a review of the latest
   SUVs, or a great place to buy laptops at a discount.
2. When you click on the link, a file transfer from a site in
   Bulgaria is initiated in the background. Files with child

pornography are then secretly downloaded to your computer. (Perhaps the extortionists use a malicious Java application that uses reverse tunneling to bypass your company's firewall.)

3. Three days later, you receive an e-mail threat. It accuses you of downloading child pornography and directs you how to find these illegal files on your computer. "Either provide a valid credit card (name, expiration date, and billing address) or we will present this evidence to your boss!"

Three out of every twelve employees will actually furnish the credit card details, but only one in twelve will report this threat to his or her employer. Other scams involve opening an attachment instead of clicking on a link. Therefore:

- Never open an incoming attachment unless it is not only from someone you know, but you are either expecting it or there is a valid explanation in the message that accompanies it.

- Never, ever, click on a link that is contained in an unsolicited e-mail from an unknown source.

HOW TO CHECK OUT A DATE OR A MATE

I trust that you, dear reader, are a straight shooter—dependable, devoted, faithful, honorable, loyal, trustworthy, truthful, upright, and kind to children and dogs. But what about that certain *other* person? What follows are some measures you can take in your defense. Let's assume the person you wish to check out is a man (such as your daughter's new love interest), but what follows can also be applied to checking out women.

USE SEARCH ENGINES

You'll need his full name, approximate age, and city of residence. Start with Google. If you have an e-mail address or a telephone number, try a search on that.

If nothing comes up, might it be he's using a fake name? Even so, you might catch him. That's what one woman I know did. She'd met a man online who seemed to be the answer to her dreams. Could he possibly be The One? She cut and pasted one of his e-mails into Google.

Bingo! The same exact words showed up on several Web sites that are dedicated to romance scams.

IF HE SENT YOU A PHOTO, CHECK IT OUT

At the very least, right click on the photo and if a menu comes up, left click on "Properties". It will tell you the date it was created. If the date is, say, ten years prior to the date you received the picture, you will have what detectives say is a "clue." In some cases (such as a picture on a Facebook page), the geotag will actually reveal the exact location where the picture was taken.

AVOID FREE DATING SITES

There are predators on paid online dating sites, too, but fewer of them. The best reason to use the paid sites is because everyone on the site had had to use a credit card, and the cards are on file. Read this warning from romancescams.org:

> The scammer . . . uses words we all like to hear to woo our hearts so they can burn our souls. They use psychology to hold you in their spell. Once they have established a relationship then the scamming begins. In all cases *the plea for financial assistance is the key to the scam*. This can be for assistance in cashing a check

that they are unable to cash themselves and also asking for financial assistance to help them out of a difficulty they are having. They have landed in a hotel and now cannot pay the bill so the hotel is holding all their papers so they cannot leave. . . . They were mugged and are in the hospital and need you to pay their hospital bill as they are being held hostage until it is paid . . .

BE ESPECIALLY WARY OF RELIGIOUS DATING SITES

The problem here is that you may trust others who contact you, believing them when they tell you they, too, are Adventist, LDS, JW, or "Christian" (whatever that means, these days). The paragraph below is an experience taken from ScamWarners.com:

> I went on ChristianMingle for online dating and was scammed. I figured it out after two weeks but not until dishing out $1,500 (which I can't believe I did) and flying to an airport to meet him and then having to wait for many hours to get a flight home. . . . When I was sitting in the airport, I received a call on my cell phone from a physician (?) who said this man had been in a car accident in which the vehicles burned but the only item salvaged was a piece of paper with my name on it. That was the trigger that this was a scam . . . I guess that I thought that a Christian dating site would be safe . . . I feel violated and ashamed . . .

Many of the LDS Web sites include excellent advice for Mormon singles who wish to meet other Mormons online. They are told to never give out personal information such as a last name, home/work addresses, phone numbers, or where they bank. They are warned never to believe everything they are told, even if it come from other LDS Web sites. Here is a typical warning:

> Ask for references, especially of family, other LDS dating friends, coworkers, or even their bishop. If you telephone one of their references, use a pay phone to avoid problems with caller ID.

Never meet alone; always bring a friend. Even for LDS dating, make sure that you meet in a public place during the day, like a mall, park, or restaurant.

The suggestion to "never meet alone" is crucial. Further, follow the advice of Canadian journalist Risha Gotlieg, who writes, "Staying local drastically reduces your chances of being scammed, since most scammers target victims outside their area to avoid being caught or prosecuted."

THREE BASIC RULES

1. Do not click on any ads you see on a Web site, including this ironic one: "Has your credit card number been stolen on the Internet? Enter it below and click 'Go' to find out."
2. Never enter accurate information into your computer or on a Web site, and especially not for an e-mail account.
3. When you sign up for whatever, use a different name, a different username, and a different password each time. Your address can be 123 Main Street, and your telephone number any area code plus 555-1212. If a Web site doesn't accept the "555" number (since 555 is invalid), feed them some other number such as that of a library or a cremation service.

MY FAVORITE QUOTE

This one's from Earl Long, the legendary governor who termed himself the "last of the red hot papas" of Louisiana politics.

Don't write anything you can phone.
Don't phone anything you can talk.
Don't talk anything you can whisper.

Don't whisper anything you can smile.
Don't smile anything you can nod.
Don't nod anything you can wink.

QUESTIONS & ANSWERS

Is it safe to store my credit card numbers on my laptop?

If you keep the number in an encrypted data file with a secure pass phrase of thirty-two alpha/numeric/punctuation mixed characters using TrueCrypt or similar, your credit card numbers should normally be safe. However, what if your laptop is stolen? Or if (unknown to you) there's a keylogger on your computer?

Personally, I prefer to keep passwords, credit card numbers, SSNs, and other sensitive information elsewhere, rather than on my computer.

Why don't you discuss anonymous methods of browsing the Internet?

Not only do they make your browsing sessions much slower, there is no real security as far as your identity is concerned. With any sort of legal problem, subpoenas will be served and your identity will be revealed. And not only that. According to a Stanford University study by the Law School's Center for Internet and Society, as reported by *The Washington Post*, most "anonymous" third-party Web tracking is not anonymous. There apparently are a number of ways in which a user's identity "can be associated with data that are supposed to be collected without linking to personally identifiable information."

Are Web-based accounts more secure than other e-mail accounts?

Web-based e-mail accounts are not more secure but they do hide some important information. They don't have a service address.

If a PI sees tuvxyz@comcast.net, for example, he has a good idea that you probably also have a television or even telephone service with Comcast. That gives him two more organizations within that company to search for a service address. (He can't do that with AOL, Yahoo!, Inbox, Bigstring, or SOS.net.)

Is there any simple way to remember complicated passwords?

This answer comes from Jon Freeman, the man even computer experts turn to when stumped. (Freeman is the owner of Barcode4.com.)

Using a different password, even just for your e-mail account, is incredibly important. I have heard of many friends and families whose computers were never infected, however their friends and acquaintances starting received phishing scams and other male enhancement ads apparently from them. They call me in a panic but the damage has already been done. "Change your password with your Internet provider right away," I tell them.

An incredibly simple system I use to make my passwords strong and easy to easily remember is use part of the business name to which they go to. For example, I use the first and last letter of the service's domain name I'm logging into at the end of my passwords. The start of my password is always uppercase, the middle lower, it contains a number, and is 9 characters long— thus it meets most website password strength requirements. So if your base strong password was "RJK&r2d" and you were logging into "Yahoo.com" you would add the letters "y" and "o." Your final password could be "yoRJK&r2d", "yRJK&r2do", or "RJK&r2dyo" depending on where you decide to put the two letters. This system works very well and ensures I have just "one" password to remember, but a different password for every system. If that system gets compromised hackers will think I'm using a strong password and give up when they try it elsewhere and it doesn't work.

For the more cautious reader, or if you're logging in from a public terminal, you can even copy/paste those two letters from the domain name into the password box after you finish typing. This will help to confuse any physical keyboard keystroke logger as they won't know you've added those two letters by mouse movement.

HOW TO LOCATE A
TRUSTWORTHY NOMINEE

As you know, an attorney filing a lawsuit may name anyone he pleases. If he is suing a corporation, he may also name the directors, the officers, and even the part-time secretary who writes the checks.

No matter how innocent you are, if you are *named* you have to defend yourself, and that costs time, money, and extreme aggravation.

So then, if you wish to remain invisible, your name must not surface anywhere. Is that difficult? Yes! But is it impossible? No, but you almost certainly cannot do this without the help of a proxy, or *nominee*. (Although the word *nominee* usually refers to a person nominated for a political office, in this book I use it in its secondary meaning: someone who takes your place as the apparent owner or manager of a company you own, or who opens a bank account for you and signs up for utilities and other services.)

Despite the tremendous advantages of using a nominee, few people are willing to do this. Some of the excuses offered are:

- "It's too much trouble."
- "I don't know who to use."
- "I don't want this additional expense."
- "I plan to get a nominee later on."

The problem with "later on" is that problems often arrive with no advance warning. What if—unknown to you—a PI has tracked you down because a lawyer is about to file a frivolous lawsuit? Or a stalker is in town, determined to do you harm? Or Homeland Security, acting on a false tip, plans to send in a SWAT team as soon as they locate your true home address?

Hopefully, nothing similar will ever happen to you, just as you may never have an accident with your car or a fire in your home. But don't you sleep better, knowing you have insurance?

ADVERTISE ON CRAIGSLIST

Most likely you are already familiar with Craigslist but if you are not, take a break here and check it out: www.craigslist.org. It is quite intuitive but if necessary, have a friend show you how to post an ad.

HOW TO INTERVIEW

One of my consulting clients is a young man in Seattle—I'll call him Mike—who planned to move from Portland to a small town east of Seattle. Following my instructions, he purchased a waterfront cabin for cash, using a New Mexico limited liability company in order to hide his ownership. Then, when ready to make the move, he advertised on the Seattle Craigslist.

"I placed my ad," Mike said, "under the title of 'Personal Assistant' in the 'Part-time' category. I didn't give out the true nature of the position in this ad although I did mention that I was 'privacy-oriented' and expected complete discretion. I asked for an educated (preferably with a liberal arts degree) person who was well-organized, professional in demeanor and appearance, had at least an average credit rating, and who was seeking part-time work."

But that was not all. Mike specified that the successful appli-cant "must have had some international travel experience, prefer-ably outside Western democratic countries. My political science background and my own travels have taught me that many Amer-icans have little understanding of how sadly lacking personal pri-vacy and security are in many countries. We just don't realize how precious our privacy really is. Travel abroad gives one a dif-ferent perspective."

Mike was dead on target when he asked for someone who had traveled or lived abroad. In my own case, had I not once lived under the dictatorship of Spain's Generalissimo Francisco Franco, I would not be working in the field of privacy today.

In the week that followed, Mike received seven responses to his ad. All were from men. He first called each applicant and briefly interviewed the candidate on the telephone. He elimi-nated three of them and arranged to interview the other four at either a coffee shop or at an inexpensive restaurant. "I got to know each applicant" he said, "through some initial small talk. I explained that my goal was to have a more private lifestyle but that everything would be absolutely, positively legal. I then handed each man a copy of *How to Be Invisible* and told him to read it. In that way, he would understand the exact lifestyle I desired. I said if he liked what he read, then he would qualify for a second interview."

All four candidates called Mike a few days later. Two said "No thanks," but the other two agreed to meet again. At this second meeting, each man was quizzed to see if he had actually read the book, and was then asked for his impression of it.

The successful candidate, Mike said, "had not only read and understood the book, but had visited both Luna's Web site and his blog and had ordered and read one of his e-books as well! The applicant was a recent college graduate who had just returned from a year of living in Eastern Europe. Our nominee arrangement began that very day."

When the terms were agreed upon, Mike drew up a simple memorandum for both of them to sign. Thus, there would be no later misunderstanding about what each had agreed to do. Mike's candidate, acting as his nominee, then undertook the following tasks, obtaining each service in his own name:

- Rent a PO box.
- Order cable TV.
- Sign up for all utilities.
- Obtain a cell phone.

HOW MUCH TO PAY THE NOMINEE

Although you may prefer to pay the nominee a flat sum to start, plus a lesser annual fee, Mike had a different plan. "I compensate the nominee for every new service he provides for me, plus reasonable expenses. For example, when he set up a PO box for me, I paid him for his time and driving expenses in addition to $120 for the annual fee of renting the box.

"For each utility, he receives the same amount as I pay. If the electric bill is $40 for the month, then I pay him $40 in cash and send a money order to the power company for the same amount. Thus, my nominee earns a 100 percent commission for every service. This doubles my costs for mail, cable, utilities, and phone but it provides a continuing incentive for him to continue."

Mike's arrangement with his nominee had now been in force for many years. When preparing this chapter, I e-mailed Mike for an update. "So far," he answered, "no problems at all. The relationship is working well."

HOW TO MAINTAIN YOUR OWN PRIVACY

Do not give a nominee your true last name, your age, your date of birth, or your previous address. This is a *business* arrangement and should always remain such.

In Mike's case, he used his true first name, but a different last name. He then programmed his cell phone with this message: "Hi, this is Mike. Please leave a message." This works well, then, for any incoming call, whether from the nominee or from a friend.

MY OWN OPINIONS AS TO USING
A STRANGER FOR A NOMINEE

I personally use longtime friends as nominees. However, were I someday to require the services of a stranger, I would—as Mike did—advertise on Craigslist. At our first meeting, if the applicant passed my initial inspection, in addition to lending him *How to Be Invisible*, I would ask for his passport. With his correct name and date of birth, I would then run Internet checks on at least these two sites:

Criminal History	http://www.criminalsearches
Check	.com/details.aspx?id=4436174
Intelius	http://www.intelius.com

If all was well, then I would set up a schedule for a one-time flat-rate fee, plus an annual fee as long as his services were used.

PROTECT YOURSELF WITH A WRITTEN AGREEMENT

The sample form below, although not drawn up by an attorney—again, I'm not a lawyer, and this book doesn't provide legal advice—is nevertheless clear and understandable. The various clauses are merely an example. Change them to suit your purposes. I strongly suggest you have your nominee sign it before a notary public. Keep the original in a safe place.

LIMITED POWER OF ATTORNEY

BE IT KNOWN, that I , [name of nominee], the undersigned, do hereby grant a limited power of attorney to [you, the reader], as my attorney. My attorney shall have full power and authority to undertake and perform the following on my behalf:

1. Make deposits and write checks on my account at [name of bank].

2. Form, amend, and cancel limited liability companies in any state.

3. Send and receive letters, instructions, and e-mails in my name.

4. Write letters, make requests, and order and receive merchandise in my name.

5. Accept payments on my behalf and sell and deliver reports on [subject of reports].

6. Engage in any other legitimate business on my behalf—including but not limited to the World Wide Web—and receive payments in my name.

7. Use funds sent to me for any purpose whatsoever.

My attorney agrees to accept this appointment subject to its terms, and agrees to act and perform in the said fiduciary capacity consistent with my best interests as he in his sole discretion deems advisable.

This power of attorney may be revoked by me at any time, provided that any person relying on this power of attorney shall have full rights to accept the authority of my attorney until in receipt of actual notice of revocation.

Signed this _____ day of _____ , 201 __ .

_____
    Signature of nominee, with name printed below.

Subscribed and sworn before me on [date] by [nominee], to me known to be the person described in and who executed the foregoing instrument and acknowledged that he executed the same as his free act and deed.

[Notary's signature and stamp.]

THE ABSOLUTE WORST FEAR FOR EVEN A LEVEL THREE PI

His worst fear is that you will move out of state and use a nominee for everything. And by everything I mean using a nominee to manage your LLCs, renting or leasing an apartment, for your landline phone, mobile phone, bank accounts, credit cards, utilities, pet licenses, cable connections, PO boxes, ghost addresses, and whatever else you need.

QUESTIONS & ANSWERS

I need a nominee for a bank account, but what's to keep him from someday just taking the money for himself?

This chapter is about locating *trustworthy* nominees. However, if you do not trust them, then maintain just enough in the nominee account to cover the checks you write. (Or, use the nominee for everything else, but keep your bank account in your own name.)

I wish to have you, Mr. Luna, furnish a nominee who will open a bank account for me. I am willing to show you my passport, give you my SSN and DOB, and give you three iron-clad references to prove that I am a solid citizen. If you wish to

*run my name on background searches, I will pay the fees. So
will you furnish a nominee for me, for everything?*

Yes, I could probably find you a rock-solid nominee, but unless
you are a millionaire, you will consider the cost to be excessive.
Below is a better suggestion:

If you have a good friend in another country, invite him or
her to come and visit you, all expenses paid. Your friend can
then open an account, sign checks, have a rubber stamp of the
signature made, and fly back home.

Or, check with your friends. One of *them* may have a trustworthy friend or relative in another country. If that person has
never before been able to afford a visit to the United States, such
an offer may be irresistible!

*NOTE REGARDING BANK CHECKS

Ideally, the imprinted checks should carry only two initials and no address. The bank's "free" checks will not
allow this, but you may be able to order such checks from
independent check printers such as CheckWorks.com or
ChecksUnlimited.com.

However, I suggest you call a representative and ask
for a form you can use to mail in your order, paying with
a temporary check from the new bank account, because
the online forms usually require a full address and a credit
card.

BANK ACCOUNTS AND MONEY TRANSFERS

Before a law firm decides to sue, they often turn the case over to a private investigator. First on his list will be to track down all your bank accounts, which he will search for state-by-state. Says a Texas PI who's read my e-book *Invisible Money*:

> Frankly, if one of your readers follows your instructions to open a no-interest account in a tiny bank in a faraway state, and does not accept a debit, credit, or ATM from that bank, I would not be able to find it. That goes for most other PIs as well—and *very few* will be more thorough than me!

That is the good news, but there's bad news to come. Did you know that financial institutions are required by the federal government to spy on their customers? The Bank Secrecy Act, which has been around for a long time, authorizes the Treasury Department to require any financial institution to report any "suspicious transaction relevant to a possible violation of law or regulation." These reports, called "Suspicious Activity Reports," are filed with the Treasury Department's Financial Crimes Enforcement Network (FinCEN). *This is done secretly, without your knowledge or consent*, any time a financial institution decides that you have done anything "suspicious."

For example, each deposit, withdrawal, exchange of currency, or other payment transfer that involves a "transaction in currency" (a physical transfer of currency from one person to another) of more than $10,000 will be reported. Reportable currency transactions include:

- Checks or drafts cashed for over $10,000.
- Cash deposits over $10,000.
- Cashier's checks purchased with cash over $10,000.
- New account opened with more than $10,000 in cash.
- Exchange of currency—small to large or vice versa; foreign to the United States or vice versa.
- Multiple cash transactions totaling more than $10,000 made in one day by or for the same person, if the bank is aware of them.

Does it appear from the above that you could safely purchase a $9,000 bank cashier's check with cash and still avoid a Suspicious Activity Report? No, because the Bank Secrecy Act also requires all banks to log purchases of any monetary instrument involving currency in the amounts from $3,000 to $10,000, inclusive. (If you happen to own a sports arena, racetrack, amusement park, licensed check-cashing service, vending-machine company, or theater, you may be exempted.)

What about foreign transactions, for an individual?

Again, a report will be made if $10,000 or more is involved, whether or not it involves cash, traveler's checks, money orders, investment securities, or negotiable instruments in bearer form.

UNINTENDED CONSEQUENCES

The information below is from an article that appeared in the
March 24, 2008, *Newsweek*:

> When Congress passed the Patriot Act, law enforcement agen-
> cies hailed it as a powerful tool to help track down the confeder-
> ates of Osama bin Laden. No one expected it would snag the
> likes of Eliot Spitzer. The odd connection between the anti-
> terror law and Spitzer's trysts with call girls illustrates how laws
> enacted for one purpose often end up being used very differ-
> ently once they're on the books. . . .
>
> The Treasury issued stringent new regulations that required
> banks themselves to look for unusual transactions and submit
> SARs—Suspicious Activity Reports—to the government. . . .
> One of these leads led to Spitzer . . . the governor called atten-
> tion to himself by asking the bank to transfer money in someone
> else's name.

And so it was that the Patriot Act unexpectedly brought down
the governor of New York—*a transfer in someone else's name*. Take
care, readers, that it never brings *you* down.

YOUR PERSONAL BANK ACCOUNT

Any bank account you have in your own name (other than the
type mentioned at the start of this chapter), tied in with your
Social Security number, can be tracked down by agencies specializing in asset searches for lawyers. This includes Certificates
of Deposit as well as IRA accounts.

Robert O'Harrow Jr., from *The Washington Post*, writes that
". . . lawyers, debt collectors and private investigators buy the data
to help in civil lawsuits, divorces, and other financial matters.

Prices range from just over $100 to several thousand dollars for a look at banks nationwide and a report that includes information about stocks, mutual funds, and safe-deposit boxes." O'Harrow relates the account of a security official at BankBoston ". . . who noticed an ad for one of the services and anonymously ordered a search on himself. When the report came back, the official, Frederick Tilley, said he learned new details about his own accounts. 'They came back with the account information, down to the penny,' said Tilley. 'There are lots of them and it's freely advertised.'"

Copies of the individual checks themselves may also be obtained, since all checks are microfilmed front and back. This reveals not only payees and endorsers but also memos (if any) and signatures.

If you are the subject of the search, what will the computers reveal? Do you wish to be identified as one with "deep pockets," or would you prefer to be considered "judgment-proof," i.e., with not enough assets worth suing you for?

Or suppose, with no forewarning, you find yourself under investigation by someone who wishes to cause you harm. This could be anyone from an ex-employee to a disgruntled present or former mate. A private detective may come up with information from so far in the past that you had forgotten it was there. Imagine that you are forced via subpoena *duces tecum*—Latin for "bring with you"—to turn over all bank records for the past three years. Are there *any* checks, *any* charges, that you would prefer to remain secret? (Think about this carefully. Consider newsletter subscriptions, contributions, trips, purchases of alcohol, guns, ammunition, or whatever. Consider rentals, from autos to motels to videos.)

Since this book is about privacy measures rather than tax evasion, you need have no secrets from the government. This report is about hiding bank accounts from your enemies, *not* from the IRS. Some of my suggestions that follow may be offbeat and perhaps underhanded. I agree, but they are not currently nor anticipated to be *illegal*, according to the attorney who reviews all my projects.

USE A NOMINEE

This method requires the assistance of a proxy or nominee— another person who will act on your behalf. Let's call this nominee Debbie E. Faith. Debbie will open a bank account in her own name. Here are the steps:

1. Choose an independent bank in a state where neither you nor Debbie lives. This will isolate both of you from routine searches and will hide Debbie's possible death (should such occur) from the bank authorities long enough for you to cash a final check, closing out all but the last $10 from the account.

2. Prepare Debbie for obvious questions such as, "Since you live in California, why are you opening this account here in Pioche, Nevada?" The answer might be "I'm thinking about moving here within the next three months." (She should have no problem saying something like that, because she can certainly *think* about it. . . .)

3. Withdraw cash from your present account(s), perhaps $1,000. Purchase a bank cashier's check from a bank where you are not known, made out to Debbie Faith and with a fictitious remitter.

4. Next, Debbie practices, hour after hour, an indecipherable signature, the kind businessmen use all over Europe. She then assembles the necessary identification (a passport is best, if she has one, since it gives far less information than a driver's license), travels to the city where the bank is lo-

cated, and opens a personal account, using any legitimate address other than where she actually lives. She will receive a minimum order of checks from the bank that will have her name and address printed in the upper left-hand corner. The checks will be mailed to the address she gave them.

5. When the printed checks arrive, tear out the two checks with the highest numbers (so it appears the account has been used), along with a printed deposit slip. You will need these to order new checks from a mail-order company such as Checks Unlimited (ChecksUnlimited.com) or Checks in the Mail (checksinthemail.com). Use one of the two checks to pay for the order, and mark the other check (sent as a sample) "VOID." Cross out both the name and address on the sample check, as well as the present number. Write in a starting number of 6001 or higher, so that the account will appear to have been established years ago. Above the deleted name and address, write in Debbie's initials "DEF." Choose a type style such as Old English that is difficult to read. Add a note somewhere to emphasize that the checks are to have *only* the initials. The mail-order check companies will usually mail only to the address printed on the sample check from your bank so it's best not to ask that they be sent to another address.

6. When the new checks arrive, Debbie sits down and signs them until her signatures start to vary. Time out for coffee or Dr Pepper, then she continues to sign, with breaks, until finished.

7. Last, but far from least, order a rubber stamp with Debbie's signature.

RUBBER SIGNATURE STAMPS

In theory, an agreement should be made with the bank in advance, before using a rubber stamp, to be able to use one as a signature on checks. In practice, however, banks seldom if ever check signatures on checks for small amounts. For a new account—such as in the example above—I suggest using checks with real signatures for the first month or so. Later, use a rubber stamp for anything below $500. Save the signed checks for times when checks must be written for larger amounts.

Incidentally, I suggest you get a rubber signature stamp for *all* your accounts, and use it from time to time just to make sure the bank is accepting them. That way you can write checks on your spouse's account, and vice versa—especially if one of you is traveling and the other is at home. About a year ago, one of my clients (I'll call him John, and his new wife Jane) followed my advice to get a signature stamp for Jane, who had a bank account in her maiden name that was used to pay utilities. Early this year, Jane had a serious illness and was hospitalized for several weeks. During this time she had worries far more serious than trying to sign checks with what would have been an unrecognizable signature. John, however, got out the stamp and continued to pay the bills in his wife's absence.

These stamps can be ordered at any office supply store, or online. I recommend Xstamper as one of the best. With this model, don't just push the top down because that might make the signature stronger on one side. Instead, position it where you want it, and then give it a firm tap in the center with your knuckles. With a few practice tries, it will work perfectly—for your nominee bank account, or for any other!

PRINT YOUR OWN CHECKS

Although I prefer the printed checks that can be ordered by mail, many of my readers say they use their computer and printer to make their own checks. There are a number of products on the market that enable the user to print the name of the account (leaving out the address), the bank information, the check number, and even the special MICR characters that can be printed with magnetic ink. A quick check on the Internet will bring up names such as VersaCheck, MySoftware, MyChecks, MyPersonal-CheckWriter, MyBusinessCheckWriter, Checknique, Cross-Check, ChecksByNow, ChecksByNet, Checker, CheckMAN, and CheckMagic. Or, purchase checks at any major office supply store.

OR, NO BANK ACCOUNT AT ALL

Hundreds of thousands of American citizens, as well as a similar number of illegal aliens, manage to live without any bank account at all, and not all are financially disadvantaged. This is one way to ensure that you do not accidentally reveal your home address by writing a check for the rent, the mortgage, utilities, taxes, or home repair.

Worse, there is a real danger if you ever write a check to a lawyer, CPA, or anyone else who—unknown to you—is a crook. When investigating this person—perhaps surreptitiously—government agents will come up with a copy of your check. Might this possibly lead to *your* mail and bank account being examined? Or a tap on *your* telephone?

Therefore, you may decide to pay professionals in cash if you're there in person. If not, you might mail a postal money order, a cashier's check, or a traveler's check. For small payments, I recommend the money orders sold in supermarkets, convenience stores, and Walmart. They are economical, can be purchased with no ID, and the line for the payee is left blank. You fill in the payee on your own. The issuing office has no record of the sender or the receiver.

For larger amounts, such as up to $2,500, you may prefer a bank money order or cashier's check. Many banks do not require ID when you are purchasing the checks with cash. If in doubt, check out a bank beforehand, asking them about their policies. Or, test their policy by purchasing a small check to pay for something you are going to order by mail. If asked for ID, tell the absolute truth: "I didn't bring any ID with me; I didn't think I'd need it."

ANOTHER GOOD REASON TO PAY CASH

Frank Abagnale, in his book *The Art of the Steal*, says on page 29:

> People can get anyone's check. All they have to do is see it. Criminals nowadays will drive around until they find a ritzy neighborhood with million-dollar homes. They'll knock on the door. When someone answers, they'll say, "Boy, you've got a lot of leaves lying on your lawn . . . I'll tell you what, my buddy and I will clean up your leaves, leave the place immaculate, and it'll cost you just seventy-five dollars." The guy thinks it's a great deal, the crooks clean up the leaves, and the owner pays them with a check for seventy-five dollars. That's all they came for: the check. Then they go to the Internet and order the checks . . . forge them, and start cashing them. Next time, the guy will rake his own leaves.

UNTRACEABLE MONEY TRANSFERS

Why not let the U.S. Postal Service move the cash for you? This is the next best way to just handing the cash over in person. As long as the recipient is also in the United States, it is perfectly legal.

HOW TO INVISIBLY TRANSFER $25,000

Obtain fifty business-size (#10) envelopes and the same number of first-class postage stamps. Pick up a magazine with lots of small pictures and price lists in the back. (Photography magazines are ideal.) Into each envelope insert five $100 bills. Wrap them in one page from the magazine. This will weigh fourteen grams, which is just half an ounce. If possible, mail the envelopes from various locations over a period of days or weeks and—if available—to multiple addresses.Remember, use normal first-class mail. Even with the cost of stamps and envelopes, this will not cost you more than $25. (I recommend you not register the envelopes. That might attract too much attention.) I've been mailing cash to others in normal envelopes for the past twenty-five years and haven't lost a dollar yet.

MAILING MONEY OVERSEAS

As long as the destination is Western Europe, there should be little if any problem as regards to safety en route. (Don't even *think* of mailing cash to Mexico or to Central or South America.) However, keep in mind the prohibition against sending $10,000 or more out of the country at any one time. Even doing it some days or weeks apart may be considered to be "structuring," which is also against the law. Now that you know this, make your own decision.

HAWALA BANKING

This is the oldest banking system in existence, used for exchanging money across international borders. Since no money actually *moves* anywhere, it cannot be traced. Although it is widely practiced among Chinese and Indians (from India), and to a lesser extent by Spaniards, the average American had never heard of it until after 9/11 (Osama bin Laden was said to use this system.)

Suppose you wish to send $25,000 from Vancouver, British Columbia, to a friend in Helsinki, Finland. You would hand $25,000 cash to a Vancouver money changer (*Hawaladar*) in Vancouver, and receive code words (or an agreed signal such as a secret handshake) and a contact address in Helsinki. No actual cash moves out of Canada. Instead, when your friend gives the code to the correspondent hawaladar in Helsinki, he will receive the equivalent in euros (less a commission) from money that is already there. To review:

- There are no written documents. The exchanges are based on mutual trust (perhaps for that reason unpopular in the United States?).
- Only *local* currencies are used. Thus, if you are sending money from the UK to Mexico, you pay in pounds and the receiver in Mexico collects in pesos.
- This exchange cannot be traced because no money crosses a border.

The *hawala* system has been under attack since 9/11 and by the time you read this it may be illegal in many countries. However, it does make for interesting conversations among friends. Beyond that, proceed at your own risk.

HOW NOT TO HAVE A SECRET ACCOUNT REVEALED

Nazita Aminpour and her husband, David, have a joint account at a Chase branch in Kew Gardens, Queens, along with a custodial one for their three children. But Nazita also had a secret bank account of $800,000—money that was apparently hers alone. Unbelievable though it seems, the suit alleges that a bank employee at Chase called David to encourage him to move some of that $800,000 in his wife's account into other investments with Chase. David knew nothing about that account until the phone call came in.

Here is what Nazita *should* have done:

1. Used a different bank.
2. Given a ghost address when she opened the account.
3. Listed a secret voice-mail number that only she could access.

Do you have a secret bank account? If so, does the banker have your true address and telephone number? If so, *move that account to another bank*!

QUESTIONS & ANSWERS

What do you think about credit unions, as opposed to banks?

In answer, I'll pass along the experience of one of my readers, who, as a college student years ago, worked in the customer service department of "one of the largest banks in the U.S." His job, as a "call center rep," was to respond to phone calls and check account data. "Not only did I have access to the customer's name, address, Social Security number, and date of birth," he writes, but "I saw every financial transaction on the account, including credit card purchases and ATM withdrawal locations."

According to my reader, there were thousands of call center reps at the bank with this kind of access. "For fun (and because we were low-paid and unethical), we'd check out the accounts of friends, lovers, coworkers, etc. Further, during late-night calls with angry/rude callers, I occasionally heard a rep reminding a caller to cool it, because we *knew where they lived*. Scary huh?" (Hopefully, of course, *your* bank has only your ghost address!) Take to heart this warning from one who knows: "Thousands of low-paid workers have access to your personal life and feel no shame in monitoring you. Remember that the next time you open an account at the big bank with the most conveniences. (*Note:* I joined a small credit union after that experience. I like to think things are a bit different there.)"

What if a bank requires my fingerprint on the back of a check?

I agree that this is an extremely irritating request, but what if your financial circumstances do not give you the option of just walking away? Keep these two points in mind:

1. As long as the check does not bounce, it will disappear into the bank archives forever.
2. If that still worries you, then try this: When you give your thumbprint, press hard and slightly twist your thumb. Practice at home first. The goal is to smear the print *just a trace*. If done right, this will make a match impossible, and yet the clerk may not notice it at all.

There is also such a thing as filling in the grooves of your thumbprint with glue, then allowing it to dry. Then a second coating is given and while still moist you press it against the thumb of another person. But I don't think you need to get into all that, unless you are on the FBI's top ten list. (And if you are, better not to cash that check at all!)

Can I pay cash to a dealer for a new car?

Not unless you are prepared to be quizzed, sign a federal form, and perhaps be reported as "suspicious" to authorities. In fact, I do not recommend ever buying a car from a dealer, new or used. Most if not all will require a photocopy of your driver's license, and sometimes your Social Security number as well.

Buy your vehicle from a private party, even if you have to travel to another state to do it. You'll certainly save money over the price of a new one. Most of the vehicles we buy are from original owners, and with 20,000 miles or less. Private parties will happily accept cash with no problem—even if you are paying $20,000 or $30,000 or more.

15

NEW MEXICO LIMITED LIABILITY COMPANIES

Mary L. was a school teacher who lived with her husband and four children near Seattle, Washington. In the early 1990s, Mary purchased a gray Volkswagen Fox. In all innocence, she titled this car in her own name. Not in her wildest dreams—or nightmares!—could Mary have foreseen the bitter consequences of driving a car with plates that would show up in the computer with her first name, middle initial, and last name.

Years passed. Unexpectedly, Mary fell in love with one of her students, a thirteen-year-old boy. Despite being married, she was unable to control her emotions. One thing led to another and Mary found herself pregnant. In 1997, the affair became known. She was arrested, jailed, and sentenced to eighty-nine months in prison. Given her lack of a criminal record and the fact she posed no threat to society, Mary was released on parole. One of the conditions of the parole was that she would not contact her young lover without permission from the authorities.

Mary carried a pager. The father of her future child, unable—

or unwilling—to stay away from Mary, sent her a page with the number of a pay phone. She called him back. That same evening she picked him up in her little gray Volkswagen Fox.

They went to a late movie, *Wag the Dog*. Then Mary parked her Volkswagen along a street near her home and they talked into the early morning hours. Mary had already packed and had hidden money and her passport in the car. They made plans to flee Seattle together and to make a new life far, far away.

At this point, was there any obstacle to their plans? The parole board had no idea that Mary was violating parole. She was not wanted by the police. No one else knew of their plans to flee. Nor was society in danger.

From Mary's viewpoint, all was well.

At 2:45 a.m., Seattle policeman Todd Harris was on a routine patrol. He passed a car that was parked along the curb. The parking lights were on. The windows were steamed up, but it appeared there were two occupants.

There was no sign of misbehavior. Nevertheless, Harris noted the Washington license plate number as he drove by. As he continued on his patrol, he ran the number through his computer to make sure the car had not been reported stolen. Several blocks later the name of the registered owner came onto the screen. The car was legally registered and was not stolen, but he recognized the name from reading about the case in the newspapers. *Mary Kay Letourneau.*

Officer Harris returned, and asked for ID. The two occupants were Mary and the boy. The boy was taken home. Mary was taken to the station, then arrested for violation of parole. On Friday, February 6, 1997, the judge revoked her parole and sentenced her to serve the full eighty-nine months. Leaving aside the morality of meeting with the father of her child, here is the lesson I want you to draw from this story: *At the time Mary titled the car*, there was not—could not have been—the slightest indication

of the troubles that lay ahead. But who among us can guarantee
that quiet waters will never see a storm?

After the Letourneau sentencing, I sent a notice to all my
clients in the United States and Canada with this headline:

SEVEN YEARS IN JAIL FOR NOT
USING A LIMITED LIABILITY COMPANY!

In neither this chapter nor the next will I be discussing all
the various uses to which limited liability companies are being
put. They have a vast application in the business, banking, partnership, and asset-protection worlds. Endless dozens of books
have been and are being written about obtaining tax identification numbers, writing complex operating agreements, registering them in other states as foreign legal entities, and opening
bank accounts here and/or abroad. All these uses are beyond
the scope of this book. From now on, when I mention LLCs, I
refer specifically to a legal entity that has all of the following
characteristics:

1. No one will know who owns it unless the owner tells
   them.
2. It will be filed in New Mexico—a state that protects privacy and does not require an annual report.
3. It will be managed by a *single member*.
4. When used (such as to buy a vehicle or real estate), it will
   list a ghost address as the principal place of business.
5. It will cost about $100 to form, and less than $100 a year
   for the resident agent (a minimum of three years is normally paid ahead).
6. The LLC name will never appear on a state or federal tax
   return.

For details, see the Appendix.

WHAT IS AN LLC?

You will sometimes hear that a limited liability company is something "new," but this refers only to the United States. In Europe, LLCs have been used for more than a century. I started using them in Spain forty years ago.

Think of an LLC primarily as a partnership, but without the liability and (now hear this!) without the necessity of actually having a partner. Like a corporation, it is a legal entity that stands alone, but it lacks the many onerous bookkeeping details and annual meetings required of a corporation.

INCOME TAX CONSEQUENCES

Since the IRS treats one-member LLCs as sole proprietorships for tax purposes, there are no income tax consequences. If you use your LLC for a part-time business, for example, you will merely report earnings and expenses on Schedule C and submit it with your 1040 tax return. *Repeat:* The income—if any—is listed on your personal tax return. Nowhere on the tax form will the name of your limited liability company appear. As far as the IRS is concerned, *your limited liability company is invisible.*

PROOF OF OWNERSHIP

"How can I prove I own the company," I'm often asked, "if my name doesn't appear anywhere?" If privacy is the goal, I recommend New Mexico LLCs because they do not show ownership in the Articles of Organization (which are a public record). The best way to prove ownership, then, is to have the original LLC documents coupled with an operating agreement. This explains who owns and operates the company. If the sole objective of the

LLC is to hold title to vehicles, an operating agreement is seldom necessary, but it is necessary for opening bank accounts as well as for holding title to real estate. This is a specialized field so I suggest you check with an attorney (see Appendix).

VEHICLE REGISTRATION DATA

The excerpt below is from Duncan Long's book *Protect Your Privacy*.

> According to the FBI, a Washington, D.C., police officer was attempting to extort $10,000 from a married man who had visited a gay bar. The officer had apparently employed a law-enforcement computer system to identify automobile license plates of cars that had been recorded as being outside the bar, and then linked the plates to the names and addresses of the vehicles. He then cross-referenced to see if the men were married, and if they were, he attempted to extort money from them. According to the FBI, the officer threatened to send photos showing the men at the bar to wives and employers if the victims didn't cough up silence money.

You may never visit a gay bar, but think of the many other dangers of allowing your name (and sometimes even your home address!) to appear on your vehicle's registration. Just one example: You innocently park in front of a home known to harbor a meth lab. You may get a visit from the police. Or perhaps the home is a so-called safe house for a Muslim terrorist cell. You may get a visit from the FBI. Or suppose the home is that of a woman who's being stalked by her insanely jealous ex-husband— you might even get beaten up!

Each of my four vehicles is titled in a separate New Mexico LLC. The address for each New Mexico LLC is overseas. We often lend our vehicles to friends. What if one of these friends would happen to park in front of the wrong home or the wrong bar? Nothing.

QUESTIONS & ANSWERS

What, step-by-step, do I have to do to buy a car and title it in an LLC?

Remember, this must be a cash purchase, and normally from a private party. (Craigslist is the best way to track down the vehicle of your choice.) Let's assume the name of your company is Ready to Go LLC:

1. There will be a box on the title for the name of the buyer to be filled in. Print "Ready to Go LLC" and then sign your first initial and last name underneath that, or just after it.
2. List the LLC's ghost address. This is where the new title will be mailed to you.
3. When the time comes to sell it, use the same information in the box for seller.

In most states, that's all there is to it. It's no different than buying or selling a vehicle in your own name. A few states, however, may present problems. California—desperate for cash!—passed a draconian law in 2011 that apparently requires all LLC owners to pay an annual $800 franchise fee. My attorney has worked out an alternate privacy solution for California residents and property using a *Privacy Trust*. Privacy trusts are more involved than LLCs, but for special situations in which an LLC won't do the trick, they can be used in every state except Louisiana. The details are too complicated to go into here, but see the Appendix on where to go for further information on this emerging privacy strategy.

HIDDEN OWNERSHIP OF VEHICLES AND REAL ESTATE

Some years back, I swung my black Jaguar sedan down the ramp and into a twenty-four-hour "high security" parking garage at Seattle's SeaTac airport, snatched the ticket stub from the attendant, raced for the shuttle bus, and just barely caught my flight to Phoenix. Eight days later I returned to SeaTac, caught the shuttle back to the garage, and joined the check-in line.

When I presented my ticket stub, the cashier hesitated.

"Sir," he said, "please step to one side. The manager will be right out."

The manager came out, introduced himself, and led me back to his office. I had visions of a scratch in the paint or a ding in a fender.

"The same day you left," he said, "your car disappeared."

"Disappeared? as in *stolen*?" (So much for the twenty-four-hour security.)

He explained that the same evening I left, one of the attendants parked a car in the stall where my car had been. When he turned the number into the cashier, the computer showed the stall was already occupied. They quickly searched the entire building to see if had been parked in another spot in error. When they failed to find it, they reported it stolen. The next morning the police spotted it, badly damaged, sitting at home plate on a baseball diamond in a Seattle park.

I have the King County Police Vehicle Impound Report before me and in the Narrative section, line 4, the officer writes, *"Unable to contact owner."* Here's why: The car was in the name of an LLC in State A. The address listed for this company was in faraway State B, and a reverse directory failed to show a telephone number at that address.

Although for many years I had been registering my vehicles in the name of limited liability companies, this was the first time my security precautions had been put to the test. No damage would have been done, of course, had the police been able to contact me in this particular case. However, a short time later my security precautions were to prove worthwhile. As soon as the insurance agent handed me a check for my Jaguar—it was too badly damaged to repair—I bought a year-old dark green Lexus (see the first question at the end of this chapter) and headed east.

A few days later I arrived in Minneapolis and spent Saturday afternoon visiting used bookstores. It was just getting dark that evening when I pulled out of a parking lot onto West Lake Street, in a hurry because I had to meet a friend from Madrid who was about to arrive at the airport. I failed to see an oncoming motorcycle and almost clipped a Harley being ridden by a 300-pound bearded bruiser. He screamed some obscenities, waved his fist, and made violent gestures to have me pull over. (If you've ever been on West Lake Street in South Minneapolis after dark, you know this is not a good neighborhood in which to pull over.)

It was too dark for the rider to see any "so-sorry" gestures— had I made them—so I fed more gas to the 290-horse engine under the hood. The overweight biker followed me right on to 35W going south, with all the time in the world to memorize my license number. Although I do not scare easily, this time I was seriously alarmed. Enough to set a new Minnesota speed record between West 35th and the I-494 junction, where I cut the lights and peeled off at the exit. Whether he memorized the number or not, and whether he was carrying a gun or not, once I lost the biker I was safe forever—the plates would lead him nowhere. But my heart was still thumping when I pulled into airport parking.

A few Saturdays later I was in Londonderry, New Hampshire, to meet Carl Prague, an old friend who used to live aboard the *Raider*, a 1912 wooden sailboat with Santa Cruz de Tenerife (Canary Islands) as a home base. A stiff wind was blowing when we stopped at the Country Market on Highway 102 to pick up some wine and snacks, and when we came out, a few abandoned shopping carts were starting to move. Just as we were putting the groceries in the car, a hard gust sent a cart racing past us and across the parking lot directly toward a parked Honda Civic with a man and a woman in it. There was no way to stop it, and we watched as it struck the driver's door with a resounding clang and bounced back. As we continued to watch, we could see that the woman was obviously screaming at the man to do something, and the "something" turned out to be a trip over to see me. Assuming he wanted some help, I lowered my window halfway as he came around my side, and said hello.

"Your cart hit my car!"

"Excuse me? We didn't have a cart."

"Yes you did, and we saw it come from here."

At least he didn't weigh more than 140, and my friend Carl is an ex-wrestler, so this time I was just amused, not scared.

"*I wrote down your license number,*" the man muttered, brandishing a scrap of paper, "and you'll hear from my lawyer."

Well, best of luck, buddy, and have a nice day.

PURCHASING A VEHICLE IN THE NAME OF AN LLC

Everything I have to say in this section makes one assumption: *You will pay cash*. I paid cash for the first car I ever bought—a 1931 Chevrolet, and I've been paying cash ever since. As long as you do not finance your purchase, taking title is usually a simple process. Nevertheless, many of my readers have been reluctant to use an LLC simply because they've never done it before.

One such person was Jim in San Francisco, who asked me to help him purchase a used Lincoln Town Car with almost no miles on it. It was for sale by a private party in Washington and Jim wanted to title it in that state for personal reasons. He asked for my help because he was not sure he could handle the registration and yet keep his name out of it. The description below is how I handled this particular transaction, step-by-step.

1. Since Jim was in a hurry, I pulled a "shelf" LLC from my files that I'll call Golden Gateway LLC. (A shelf LLC is one that has been formed in the past for future use, and just put "on the shelf" until needed. I recommend this procedure to all readers, and I personally keep shelf LLCs on hand at all times. The ones I have all show an address in Spain as their principal place of business.) We then flew to Seattle, rented a car, and drove out to Port Angeles to make the deal.

2. The seller, a ninety-seven-year-old (!) woman who had purchased the car in 1991 and then stored it, signed off on the title. She also signed the bill of sale I had prepared beforehand. We filled in "Golden Gateway LLC" as the buyer and gave a ghost address that Jim had already arranged for beforehand.

3. Rather than go to the Department of Motor Vehicles in Port Angeles, we went to a private licensing bureau. (They charge a small fee for handling the paperwork, but the lines are shorter and they are sometimes easier to deal with than

clerks at the DMV.) Jim went through the line with me, but only as an observer. He wanted to see how I would answer the questions. (He had arranged for the LLC's address to be a ghost address in Alaska.)

Clerk: What's the UBI number for this company? (Washington requires an ID number for all legal entities doing business in their state.)

Me: Golden Gateway LLC doesn't do business in this state, and Alaska doesn't require a UBI number.

Clerk: Then why not license it in Alaska?

Me: For at least six months the car will be in this state, and the law requires we therefore license it here. (100 percent correct, in all states.)

She then pushed a computer printout over to me and showed me where to sign. I scrawled an illegible signature that matched the one on the bill of sale (although she didn't ask to see it).

Clerk: Print your title after your signature, please.

Since I was neither a member nor a manager of Jim's newly acquired company, I wrote in "Sales Mgr." (Jim retroactively appointed me "Sales Manager for a Day.") We paid the various license and transfer fees in cash and were on our way. The title arrived at Jim's ghost address in Fairbanks and was sent on to him, as were all annual registration notifications.

> *Note:* If you run into trouble, don't make a scene. Stay calm and leave if necessary. So much has to do with the person you're dealing with. Consider ways around the roadblock and try again another day at a different office or with a different clerk.

WHAT WAS ACCOMPLISHED?

First and foremost, *total privacy*. Suppose a private investigator sees Jim's car parked in Las Vegas at what he considers a suspicious address, and obtains whatever information is on file with the DMV in Olympia, Washington. He will get the name "Golden Gateway LLC" and Jim's ghost address in Alaska. If the PI then checks with the secretary of the commonwealth in Juneau, he will learn that it is not an Alaskan company. He'll then check with Olympia. No, not a Washington company, either. That leaves him forty-eight states plus the District of Columbia to check out. The search usually ends right there.

However, assume the PI continues doggedly on and eventually does do a search of New Mexico's database. All he will find there is an address in Spain.

INSURING YOUR VEHICLE

The easiest—and recommended—way to obtain insurance is to use your own name. This will keep your rates low, especially when you have multiple vehicles titled in separate LLCs. As far as I have been able to learn, this will not compromise your privacy because only the LLC name will show up on the registration.

CHOOSING A NAME

It's often fun for the whole family when it comes to choosing suitable names for the various LLCs that will be used for future purposes.

North Dakota Sodbusters LLC	family home
Victoria's Sea-Crate LLC	SeaSport cabin cruiser

King of the Road LLC	husband's Dodge Ram 3500
Her Royal Majesty LLC	wife's Toyota Highlander
One Cool Chick LLC	daughter's Mazda Miata
Road Less Traveled LLC	son's Jeep Wrangler

All of the above could, of course, be titled in a single limited liability company to keep costs down. The main problem to having everything in the same LLC is the protection you lose if a PI is on the trail of your assets. Let's say that in the example above, everything is titled in King of the Road LLC.

If a PI comes up with the driver of any one of the vehicles and checks the plate, he'll follow this with a search for anything owned by King of the Road LLC. What will he find? All the other vehicles, the boat, *and the address of the family home.*

HIDDEN OWNERSHIP OF YOUR HOME

What I had to say about paying cash for your car also applies to real estate. (By "cash," I don't mean paying in $100 bills, I mean not taking out a mortgage.) Give your attorney—or the title company—a copy of the Articles of Organization, along with clear instructions that your name is to appear only in their office files, and not on any public database.

However, if you plan to finance your home, then the mortgage company is going to demand that you guarantee the loan in your own name, which means using an LLC will not help. (Until I was sixty years old, we lacked the cash to buy a home outright, so we always rented . . . and saved some money as well. As talk show host Bruce Williams used to preach, "Renting is cheaper than buying.")

QUESTIONS & ANSWERS

You mentioned driving a Jaguar, but doesn't that draw undue attention to yourself?

I confess that from an early age I've had a weakness for upscale cars—Packards in the old days, and in later years Mercedes, Jaguars, and Lexus. However . . . it's never too late for common sense. Thus it was that just one month after the second edition of this book went to press, your humble servant stepped down to a used Toyota pickup. My wife followed suit by selling her Lincoln Continental and buying a used Camry. Now that we've finally set the right example (with four "vanilla" vehicles), here are some reasons why I suggest you follow suit.

- You'll save some serious money. Less initial cost, less depreciation, less money at the gas pump, and a lower insurance rate.
- You'll no longer be the subject of envy by your less-fortunate neighbors, relatives, and friends.
- You'll no longer be a prime target for carjackers or burglars. (Burglars have been known to spot a luxury car and follow it home. Later, when the owner leaves, they break into the home, assuming that valuables must be there.)
- You'll have more privacy as you travel about, blending in with hundreds of similar vehicles on the road.

What about long trips? In our case, we prefer a heavy car with lots of room when we're going to be driving for many hours, so we rent a Lincoln from Hertz. Not only is this cheaper than owning the car, there is an additional advantage. If the car should break down or be involved in a fender-bender far from home, Hertz just delivers another Lincoln and away we go.

I just moved from Denver to Miami. Since I am keeping my Colorado driver's license, should I also keep my Colorado license plates?

Not unless you also get Florida plates. Les L. is one of my clients. Les works for a well-known electronics company in California's Silicon Valley. He also happens to live there, but he licensed his new Porsche in Texas (for the tax savings) and obtained a Texas driver's license. He does have a ghost address in Texas, and he knows the area around Plano.

One day he was stopped and questioned by the California Highway Patrol. The officer did not accept his story of being from Texas. He was ordered to obtain California plates within thirty days or face a serious penalty. Rather than accept this, Les went to court.

"I'm a Texas resident," he said. "The officer made a mistake. Here is my Texas driver's license with my Texas home address." The judge accepted this explanation and Les kept his Texas plates. Two months later, Les was in a commuter parking lot taking a nap in his car.

"A cop woke me up and was suspicious of the Texas plates despite my Texas driver's license. He asked me a lot of questions about what I was doing and how long had I been out here. I simply said, 'I'm a Texas resident working out here temporarily.' He called it in and everything was okay, so he left me alone."

However, here's what happened later:

"I was pulled over by a traffic cop who was part of a special task force with access to a database that records license plates whenever exiting airport garages or crossing toll bridges. He was able to immediately determine that the car had been in California for longer than the allowed period of time. The car was immediately impounded and I was left standing on the curb looking for a taxi. Cost me eight hundred dollars to get the vehicle back."

If one of the bad guys takes down your license plate number, what can you do?

I will not list the variety of legal reasons for which you may suddenly wish to change your license plate number. I will, however, cite a recent example that involved one of my consulting clients. (Names have been changed.)

David White spent a long evening at the home of Maria Flores, an attractive young Mexican widow who lives in a village nearby. His beige Camry was parked in her driveway. When the time came to leave, David opened Maria's front door, snapped on the outside light, and spotted two men at the back of his car. One was holding a flashlight and the other had a pad and pencil in his hand. David yelled and reached into his jacket as if to withdraw a handgun. Both men fled. He called me at sunrise the next morning and asked me what to do.

"I need to keep using my car, but these guys have got my license plate number."

"It can't be traced, David." (Following my instructions, the car had been titled in the name of a New Mexico LLC with a ghost address.)

"But these guys and their pals will be watching for it."

"I'll meet you down at the licensing bureau when they open," I said. "You'll get new plates that show you contribute to a law-enforcement memorial. You'll pay an extra forty dollars a year, but you'll have a new number and will get the vanity plates right away."

I keep a drawer full of decals and bumper stickers for every occasion, and I selected one before heading out to meet David. His car now has a new license plate with a silhouette of some law-enforcement officers on the left side, and also a prominent decal in one corner of the rear window noting the following:

FRATERNAL ORDER OF POLICE
ACTIVE SUPPORTER

Will having license plates that cannot be traced protect me from stalkers?

You mean, like, "guaranteed?" When it comes to privacy and security, there are few if any guarantees, but the precaution you mention will certainly balance the odds in your favor. However, if someone seems to be able to mysteriously track you down after a "foolproof" move, perhaps he followed your U-Haul trailer or truck when you moved. Some stalkers have trailed their victims from one coast to the other. Or perhaps:

- He found out where your children go to school, and followed them home.
- He followed you home from work, church, or a visit to a relative.
- He followed you home from the airport.
- He requested a hearing, forcing you to show up in court, then followed you home.

The only sure way to avoid being followed is to never be located in the first place. If you have to meet with the stalker for any reason whatsoever, he certainly may attempt to follow you. Then again, ask any private investigator who the toughest person is to follow, and he'll tell you that it's the target who is *aware*. Perhaps not conscious of any specific thing, but just alert in general. Looking around when walking, watching the mirrors when driving, etc.

Carjackers say the same thing—many crimes would have been avoided had the victims been aware of their approach. In my own case, I never allow any specific car to follow me for a period of time in rural areas (where our homes usually are). I drive a few miles over the speed limit, and if a car comes up behind me I turn on the right-turn signal, slow down, and force him to pass.

If you live in a city and think a certain car is following you, make four consecutive right or left turns, i.e., go around the block. If the car you've seen in your mirrors follows you, *do not go home.* Drive to the nearest police or fire station or to a well-lighted gas station with a number of cars filling up. Hopefully you will have your cell phone with you, in which case you can dial 911.

What precautions can be taken against carjackers?

Privacy and security go together. In the words of the Los Angeles Police department—referring to carjackings—"Don't give up your privacy." In other words, *never* get into your own car at gunpoint. Just pretend to faint (or maybe for real!) and fall down limp.

Here's a scam I hear about from time to time. It's an oldie, but it still works. The latest is a report about a BMW that was parked late at night outside an upscale restaurant in Marin County, California. Someone called the restaurant to report that there was a white BMW 740i in the parking lot and its lights were still on. When the owner showed up (and of course the lights were *not* on), he was robbed at gunpoint and his car was taken.

Female drivers, when alone, attract more attention than males. One solution is to tint your windows as dark—or darker—than the law allows. Then have a male mannequin in the passenger seat. In fact, with dark enough tinting you may even get by with one of those rubber masks from a costume store. Just slip it over the headrest—can't hurt, might help. (Just don't use this gag for the carpool lane, however. You may stumble across a cop with less than an adequate sense of humor.)

While on this subject, below is an article from the *Skagit Valley Herald,* titled "Accused Rapist Had Been Jailed."

According to police, the man rammed his car into the woman's vehicle about 7 p.m. Wednesday. The woman later told police she got out and the man then pushed her into his own car, climbed in, and drove south . . . he beat her up and raped her.

Hint to you, husbands: Note the words *"she got out."* Might this be a good time to review security with your wife, and make sure she always keeps her car doors locked and has her cell phone with her?

17

LAPTOP COMPUTERS

Gone are the days when you need a desktop computer for computing power. I suggest laptops only because they are so much more convenient to conceal.

I take precautions that many of you readers have never dreamed of, yet never for a moment do I fool myself into thinking that the data on my computer is secure. And take note—this chapter discusses neither e-mail nor the Internet. It deals only with a personal, non-networked computer that is never, ever connected to any medium outside the four walls of your home.

Perhaps you have a file or a folder that you wish to keep private because it contains personal letters, financial records, business secrets, pictures, a list of confidential names and addresses, or whatever. Here are some of the ways in which such information could be obtained by others:

- A family member or friend (perhaps of your teenaged children) checks out some of your personal files.
- A thief breaks into your home, steals the computer, and sells it through a fence who in turn sells it to—who knows?

- The local police get a search warrant based on a false complaint and confiscate your computer. Even though you are later proved innocent, they'll check your hard drive in the meantime with a killer program called EnCase.

- A PI will park his van down the street and—thanks to the "van Eck" emissions from your monitor—will read everything on your screen. *Legally*.

- The FBI targets you for some ephemeral reason, but does not have hard evidence to obtain a warrant. Instead, they do a *sneak and peak*, a surreptitious entry to check out the hard drive on your computer. Before they leave, they'll install a *keylogger*, which will record every keystroke you make from then on, *including passwords* . . . and you'll never be the wiser.

Do not travel with this laptop. (Use a second "clean" laptop for the Internet, and for when you travel.) More than 700,000 laptops are stolen every year while traveling or commuting. Some are left in taxis by mistake. Some disappear after leaving them too long at the far end of the airport scanning machines. Others are stolen from hotel rooms, or snatched at the airport when the owner set his laptop down for "just a moment."

ENCRYPTED FILES

For many years I resisted all forms of encryption, assuming that it was either too much trouble, or beyond my capabilities. However, with the help of my PI friend Tim LaTrasse, all my laptops are now encrypted, as well as many of my flash drives. I asked Tim to write a short e-book with instructions so basic that even his grandmother could follow them. By the time you read this, his e-book should be available at CanaryIslands Press.com.

HIDE YOUR LOCATION

As often mentioned in this book, no one outside your close friends and (perhaps) relatives should know where you live. If investigators cannot find you, they cannot alter, add to, or confiscate your computer. (The same applies if you work in a private office away from home. If you fear surreptitious entry, take the laptop with you when you leave.)

FORTIFY THE ROOM WHERE YOU WORK

This is your second layer of defense. Gerry L., a close friend of mine for the past forty-five years, writes and sells computer programs for small businesses all over Spain. He has a suite of rooms in a high-rise office building on Tenerife Island with a single entrance door. The outside of this door appears normal, but it is backed on the inside with a steel plate. When locked, a remote signal slides iron bars across the back. All windows face the open sea, which protects him against monitoring by laser, and he uses only laptops with screens and fonts designed to foil anyone trying to monitor the low-level radiations.

At home, of course, a steel entrance door may be of little help because of all the windows. However, if your computer is in a room in the basement or on an upper floor, why not install a reinforced door? If you add a keyless electronic access control, you may be able to thwart PIs and/or government agents despite their lock-picking tools and skills.

Often, however, the computer will be kept in a ground-floor

guest bedroom that is being used as a home office. If you have a desktop computer, hooked up to one or more printers and perhaps a scanner as well, you won't want to move it every time you leave the house empty for a short time. In this case, you may wish to install a long narrow table across the back of the closet, and then have a carpenter install secure doors that can lock everything inside.

DO NOT TRUST YOUR NEIGHBORS

Jim and Jane B——, a young working couple with no children, had long planned on a two-week trip to Hawaii. When the time came to leave, they left a key to their home with Jane's brother, Karl. This was to be used only in the case of an emergency.

Upon their return they picked the key up from Karl and all seemed to be well. Several months passed. One evening, when they returned home from work, they found the computer turned on. Jim was positive it had been off since the previous evening. Alarmed, he checked the history and the cookies and found a sea of child pornography Web sites! He checked all the windows and doors. No trace of a break in. Jane checked the drawer in her nightstand. The money she kept there had not been touched. This had all the markings of an inside job by someone who had a key.

Karl, when contacted, was persuaded to avoid a serious beating by confessing. He'd copied the key they had once left him and had been slipping into their home to use the computer while Jim and Jane were away at work. When an emergency call had come in on his cell phone, in his haste to leave he'd forgotten to clear the history and the cookies and to also turn off the computer.

If you are ever caught in such a situation, the first thing to do is to back up the files you need and then destroy the hard drive.

Sand the surface of the disk with a belt sander, melt it down, or hammer it into tiny pieces and then feed them slowly into a fast-moving river. Otherwise, what remains on that drive could someday be used against you.

As for leaving a key behind, here is how we do it when we will be absent for a period of time. A key is hidden outside in such a way that not even the Homeland Security boys will ever find it. If an emergency should ever come up (and so far it never has), our neighbor Maggie has instructions to call my cell number and leave a message. I will then call her back and describe in detail the hidden location of the key. Maggie is in her eighties and doesn't know a modem from a monitor. In fact, she'll never *see* the computers because I leave them in an undetectable secret room.

WHAT ABOUT THE FOURTH AMENDMENT?

The Fourth Amendment to the U.S. Constitution states:

> The right of the people to be secure in their persons, houses, papers, and effects, against unreasonable searches and seizures, shall not be violated, and no Warrants shall issue, but upon probable cause, supported by Oath or affirmation, and particularly describing the place to be searched, and the persons or things to be seized.

With respect to criminal prosecution, the amendment applies solely to "the State" and agents of the state. Therefore, if a non-law-enforcement person sneaks into your home and finds what appears to be incriminating evidence, it can be turned over to the police and will probably be admissible in court. The court will want to make sure, of course, that the evidence was obtained without a suggestive direction from law enforcement such as, "We think there might be some evidence in that place but (*wink-wink*) we're not allowed to go get it."

PASSWORDS

If you encrypt a file with a password, you should know that computer forensic experts use password-cracking programs that can pull up any real word *in any language*. A good friend once used one of these programs to attack a secret file that was protected by a nine-digit password, author unknown. When the English program failed, he went to Spanish, then French, then German, then Italian. The seventeenth language he tried was Pakistani, and the password that unlocked the code turned out to be the name of a relative in Pakistan.

Never store your passwords in your wallet, purse, or a sticky note on the bottom of a desk drawer. Also, be very careful about those password-hint options at Web sites. Make sure the hint won't be a giveaway to those who know you well. For example, if the question is about your mother's maiden name, choose a totally different name and memorize it.

In addition, form the habit of never, ever using a real word by itself. Instead, use a phrase. Key in the first letter of each word, followed by an actual word at the end. Eight digits should be your minimum; twelve is better. *Example*: The phrase "I was born and raised in Dakota" translates to iwbarid.

Next, substitute a symbol for one of the vowels. In the example just given, let's change the "a" to "@." Then capitalize the last letter. We now have iwb@riD. Add a four-digit number, perhaps some obscure historical date such as "0654" or "1040." Any password formed in this matter should certainly be secure . . . or will it?

Veronica V., a professional paranoid, has a secret office in her home that has triple locks and is protected against CO_2-laser-reflective sound being picked up from the window. (She keeps a small massage vibrator on the windowsill, behind the screen, where it can touch the glass.) Two vicious Dobermans patrol the yard behind a chain-link fence.

Veronica—expert in the use of encryption—now compiles a list of names and addresses for a secret mailing list. She protects this list by using PGP encryption that she has compiled herself. She makes sure she's running a clean version and she chooses as her password "1latfar1ghts1215." She commits this password to memory ("I love all those Fourth Amendment rights," substituting the number "1" for the letter "i" and adding a date) so that no one can ever find it even if she's raided. She never encrypts a message while online, so no one can monitor the data line. She even wipes her swap file so there'll be no trace of the password anywhere.

No one, *no one*, she vows, will ever get this password out of her unless they clip wires to her most sensitive parts and crank up the voltage. And, since she lives in the good ol' USA instead of Mexico, Israel, or North Korea, torture (aka "rubber-hose cryptography") is not an option.

Nevertheless, unless Veronica protects herself against the dreaded "Tempest" as well, her so-called secret password can be plucked from the air with not so much as a nod to the Dobermans.

TEMPEST AND VAN ECK

Although these two terms are sometimes used interchangeably, they are not the same thing. TEMPEST is a set of standards used by the government to gauge and reduce electromagnetic emanations from electronic equipment. The radiations themselves are often referred to as "van Eck" radiations, named after Dutch scientist Wim van Eck who published an unclassified paper on the subject back in 1985.

TEMPEST frequencies run from commercial AM stations to the upper reaches of 600 MHz, and thus cover transmissions from your TV set, your stereo system, your microwave oven, your wireless alarm system, your cordless phone, *and your computer*. Your monitor acts as a radio transmitter, sending out signals in the 2 to 20 MHz range. (These resemble broadcast TV signals, although various forms of sync will require restoration.)

So then, your keyboard strokes are transmitted into the air. Any digital oscilloscope, in the hands of a professional, can detect the leaking signals with ease. Therefore, when Veronica types in her password, the man with the van Eck receiver in the Ford van down the street sees that password magically appear on his screen!

Your printer, too, can betray your privacy. The NSA uses a classified technique called *digram analysis* to assist in eavesdropping on van Eck emanations from printers. Remember, all monitoring of your equipment is passive, and therefore cannot be detected. Unless you take protective measures, an information warrior can, with the proper frequency tuning, antenna manipulation, reintroduction of sync and vehicle location, monitor you anyplace, anywhere, anytime.

> *Warning:* If you live in a terrorist country and are composing a list of freedom fighters, obtain and study the book *Desktop Witness*, by Michael A. Caloyannides. If you think that mere encryption will solve your problems, Caloyannides will disabuse you of that notion.

QUESTIONS & ANSWERS

How can I dispose of an old hard drive?

If possible, do something similar to what they do in the Marine Corps: sand the top off with a belt sander. Or burn it. At the very least, hammer it into bits and pieces and then drop them off a bridge.

Couldn't a PI who secretly enters my home to install a key-logger be prosecuted for trespass?

In theory, yes, but according to both a detective I spoke with, and a Harvard-trained prosecutor, since the question is about prosecution criteria, the answer is almost invariably no. Trespass is a minor crime that a prosecutor will seldom mess with, knowing that even if he does file, jurors will seldom convict.

Where should I buy a new laptop?

You might try Best Buy or one of the office supply stores. If you order online, use someone else's credit card and hand them the money—plus a little extra—up front. (In this case, the computer may have to be shipped to their address, but if not, use your ghost address.) And when you boot up for the first time and must fill in some blanks, don't even think of using your own name. (You can often get by with an "x" or a zero.)

What if I forget my password and thus lose a file I really need?

The protection against losing a password is to use a personal fin-gerprint reader such as that found at www.digitalpersona.com. These readers convert your print into a unique digital string that becomes your password. Just don't lose that finger!

THE DANGERS OF
FACEBOOK ARE REAL

I have a great advantage over the young people of today. Why? Because I can compare the days before Mark Zuckerberg's father was born, to these days when Mark's creation blankets the world. Along with others who grew up during the Great Depression, I remember when we had time to think.

"The great omission in American life," writes author Marya Mannes, "is solitude . . . that zone of time and space, free from the outside pressures, which is the incinerator of the spirit."

"In so many ways we, as a people, have declared war on solitude and meditation," said Simeon Stylites in the December 1, 1954, *Christian Century*. "The worst possible calamity is to be alone. If you enjoy anything alone, you are 'antisocial' and ought to be rushed to the psychoanalyst's couch, or better still to the mental hospital."

"We seem so frightened today of being alone," wrote Anne Morrow Lindbergh in her book *Gift from the Sea*, "that we never let it happen. . . . Certain springs are tapped only when we are alone. The artist knows he must be alone to create; the writer, to work out his thoughts; the musician, to compose; the saint, to pray."

LACK OF PRIVACY

Do people really have privacy on Facebook? There are all kinds of ways third parties can access information about you. Ever played any popular games on Facebook, such as Farmville? Ever taken any of those popular quizzes? Every time you have, you authorized an application to be downloaded to your profile. That in turn gave your information to third parties.

ACQUAINTANCES VS. FRIENDS

Remember that old high school bully who made your life miserable? Or that creepy classmate who told lies about you behind your back? And people like this now want to be your *friend*? How many true friends do we normally have in life? Can you count them on one hand, or two hands at most?

When someone claims to have 1,000 friends, do you really want to be 1 of the 1,000?

SIX LEVELS OF ADDICTION

"Facebook Addiction Disorder" [FAD] is a condition in which the healthy balance of an individual's life is adversely affected by excessive amounts at time spent on Facebook. It has been said that approximately 350 million people are suffering from the disorder. According to many psychologists, if a person displays at least two to three of the following criteria during a six- to eight-month time period, he or she is a victim of the condition.

1. **Tolerance:** The person needs increasing amounts of Facebook time in order to obtain satisfaction. A sign to look out for is having multiple Facebook windows open. Three or more is a clear warning.

2. **Withdrawal symptoms:** These become noticeable when victims are restricted from using Facebook because they have to participate in normal everyday activities. Common signs are anxiety, distress, and the obsessive need to talk about Facebook and what might have been posted on their wall in their absence.

3. **Reduction of normal social/recreational activities:** Facebook addicts reduce the time spent catching up with friends, playing sports, or pursuing hobbies, simply to spend time on Facebook. In extreme cases, the person will even stop answering a parent's phone calls, instead insisting that friends and relatives use Facebook to contact them.

4. **Virtual dates:** It is obvious that things are out of hand when real dates are replaced with virtual dates. Instead of going to the movies or out to dinner, a Facebook addict will tell a girlfriend or boyfriend to be online at a certain time.

5. **Fake friends:** If eight out of ten people appearing on their Facebook page are complete strangers, they have a serious case of FAD.

6. **Complete addiction:** When serious Facebook addicts meet new people, they tend to say their name, followed by "I'll talk to you on Facebook." Even their pets have Facebook pages. Any notifications, wall posts, inboxes, or friend requests give FAD victims an addict's "high," much like the highs felt by gambling addicts.

A PROBLEM WITH NO EASY SOLUTION

"I hate having my picture taken," wrote "Camera Shy" to Jeanne Marie Laskas in a November 2011, *Reader's Digest* article. "People always make me feel as though I'm in the wrong if I refuse to pose or get in a group photo. These shots always end up on social networking sites without regard for people's feelings or privacy. How do I explain that I don't want my picture, or my baby's picture, to be taken and posted online?"

Laskas is one of the sharpest knives in the advice-giving drawer, but not even she had a solution to that one, other than telling Camera Shy not to be caught doing something "stupid" when her picture was taken.

UNINTENDED CONSEQUENCES

On October 11, 2006, Joshua Lipton, a twenty-year-old college junior, was driving under the influence of alcohol. As a result, he injured a woman in an accident. Lipton was not jailed at the time, but a court hearing was set for a later date. Two weeks later he attended a Halloween party dressed as a prisoner. Pictures from the party showed him in a black-and-white striped shirt and an orange jumpsuit labeled "Jail Bird." So far, not good. It gets worse. An unknown "friend" who was also at the party took some pictures of him and posted them on his or her Facebook page.

Enter Jay Sullivan, the prosecutor handling Lipton's drunk-driving case. He (or someone under his direction) searched Facebook and found Lipton's pictures. When the case came to trial, Sullivan used the pictures to paint Lipton as an unrepentant partier who lived it up while his victim recovered in the hospital. The judge agreed, calling the pictures depraved when sentencing Lipton to two years in prison.

Note: I make no defense for Lipton or for anyone else who drinks and drives. The point here is that whoever posted Lipton's picture on Facebook had no thought of the unintended consequences. The results of such thoughtless actions can cause the loss of someone's job, the breakup of a marriage, or even rape and murder. In the case of young women, sometimes it's the victim herself who fails to foresee where her foolish choice may lead.

SEXTING CAN LEAD TO SEXTORTION

INDIANA. At a party with a webcam, three teenage girls visited an Internet chat room. One thing led to another, and the boys on the other end dared them to flash their breasts. They did, but no problem, right? The boys were in some other state, far away, and they'd never hear from them again.

A week passed. Then one of the girls received a series of threats by e-mail. She was told to either e-mail more explicit pictures and videos of herself, "or I'll post your pictures to all your MySpace friends."

Did the girl then confess to her parents what she had done?

No, she complied with his demand at least twice. (Police and federal authorities eventually became involved and indicted a nineteen-year-old Maryland man for the crime of "sextortion.")

SEXTORTION IS INCREASING

Teens are more vulnerable to blackmail because they're easy to intimidate and embarrassed to tell their parents. The result is that they will do almost anything to keep naked pictures of themselves from getting out.

ALABAMA. Jonathan, twenty-four, extorted nude photos from more than fifty young women who were on Facebook or MySpace.

WISCONSIN. Anthony, eighteen, posed as a girl on Facebook to trick male high school classmates into sending him nude cell phone photos, which he then used to extort them for sex.

CALIFORNIA. A thirty-one-year-old man hacked into more than 200 computers and threatened to expose nude photos he found unless their owners (many of them juveniles) posed for more sexually explicit videos.

Here is a suggestion to any of you parents with a teen daughter. Have a serious talk with her about the dangers of sexting. Explain that if, despite your warnings, she takes some revealing pictures of herself and sends them to anyone on the planet Earth, she may soon get a threat to take and send more pictures, *or else.* Kindly explain to her that she will at this point have two options:

Plan A. She can confess to you and ask for your help. There will be some consequences such as grounding involved, but this will pass and you love her and will help her and protect her.

Plan B. Instead of coming to you, she can submit to the threats and send the blackmailer whatever he asks for. Explain that this will eventually come to light anyway and at *that* point, life as she's known it will disappear.

ON FACEBOOK, NO ONE KNOWS WHO YOU REALLY ARE

As you read the following account from the UK, think about whether or not the mother should have (a) allowed her daughter to be on Facebook at all, or (b) allowed her to have a Facebook page but monitored her page every day, or (c) just trusted her daughter to be careful.

Ashleigh Hall, seventeen, met Peter Cartwright, nineteen, on Facebook. They quickly became friendly, exchanging notes on their walls and then sending text messages to each other. From the bare-chested picture posted on his profile, Peter was seen to be an attractive young man. Within a month, Peter convinced Ashleigh to meet him face-to-face. To do so on a certain Sunday evening, the girl told her mother she was going to stay with a friend. Then she headed out to meet Peter near Sedgefield, County Durham.

Peter's last name was actually Chapman. He was a bald, geeky-looking thirty-three-year-old registered sex offender missing most of his teeth. Ashleigh was one of the 6,000 "friends"—all women—he was in contact with through ten social networking sites. But once Ashleigh met this revolting creature, wouldn't she scream and run? No, because Peter had told Ashleigh that *his father*, driving a Ford Mondeo, would pick her up and take her to him. Thus the girl entered Peter's car willingly, suspecting nothing. Chapman kidnapped her, raped her, then strangled her and dumped her lifeless body in a farmer's field near Sedgefield, County Durham, near a known lovers' lane.

Repeat sex offender Peter Chapman is currently doing life in prison, but this brings little comfort to Ashleigh's mother. *If only she'd kept her daughter out of Facebook!*

EMPLOYERS TRACK DOWN OLD POSTS AND PICTURES ON FACEBOOK

According to a 2009 survey conducted by Microsoft, 79 percent of hiring managers and job recruiters in the United States review online information about prospective employees, and 70 percent of those surveyed said they've actually rejected applicants based on their findings. Similarly, negative posts about your current job, employer, or coworkers could lead to you being fired.

"MORE YOUTHS SEEING THEIR FACEBOOK, E-MAIL HACKED"

The above headline is from the Kim Komando newsletter on October 10, 2011. The article discusses the problem many teens face—that of their friends having or figuring out their passwords and then posting embarrassing messages on their page. As one girl said, "I was really confused about how they got my password," she said. "I felt violated." Most amusing, however, were the comments about Josie Burris:

> Josie Burris, sixteen, says she's shared her Facebook password with her best friend as well as her boyfriend. Once, she spied on her boyfriend's page to peek at his private messages and "see what he was up to . . ." She says her parents are on Facebook, too, but she doesn't worry about them spying on her.
>
> "I make sure I don't put anything bad on there," she said, but added: *"Old people shouldn't have Facebook. I firmly believe in that (italics added)."*

MY FINAL WORD ON THIS SUBJECT

To paraphrase Josie: *"Young people shouldn't have Facebook. I firmly believe in that."*

QUESTIONS & ANSWERS

How many profiles on social media are fake?

It's been said that at least 30 percent of the profiles on social media are fake, but that may be higher by the time you read this. A large number of fake profiles are set up by . . . (wait for it) . . . the U.S. government. Check out www.examiner.com (February 17, 2011), "US Gov. Software Creates 'Fake People' on Social Networks" (www.examiner.com/social-media-in-national/us-gov -software-creates-fake-people-on-social-networks-to-promote -propoganda).

What about using Facebook for business only? And what about MySpace, Google+, Twitter, Pinterest, and LinkedIn?

This chapter is about personal use of social media, especially by teens that are online without parental permission or controls. It is about the dangers of predators, viruses, lower productivity, narcissism, and the ever-present possibility of ending up with short attention spans.

As for business, such sites may be useful. None of our children use any social networks personally, but our youngest daughter does use Facebook for her business. Also, my webmaster is pushing me to use Twitter because of "recent improvements in Twitter's privacy and security controls." So . . . I may be on Twitter by the time you read this.

19

THE ART OF PRETEXTING, AKA SOCIAL ENGINEERING

Earlier in this book, I discussed a way in which to hire reliable and trustworthy people to clean any office away from home. However, unless you drill certain rules into the heads of everyone on the job, your workers could innocently make a terrible mistake. The following true account comes from Kevin Mitnick's book, *The Art of Deception*. A man Mitnick calls Ned Racine decided to raid the offices of one of his clients. The objective was to steal valuable information to help the client make a killing in the stock market.

For a few days in a row, Ned kept watch on the parking lot of the small business park where the accounting company has its unpretentious store-front-like offices. Most people left between 5:30 and 6:00. By 7, the lot was empty. The cleaning crew showed up about 7:30. Perfect.

The next night at a few minutes before 8 o'clock, Ned parked across the street from the parking lot. As he expected, the lot was empty except for the truck from the janitorial services company. Ned put his ear to the door and heard the vacuum cleaner running. He knocked at the door very loudly, and stood there waiting in his suit and tie, holding his well-worn briefcase. No answer, but he was patient. He knocked again, A man from the cleaning crew finally appeared. "Hi," Ned shouted though the glass door, showing the business card of one of the partners that he had picked up some time earlier. "I locked my keys in my car and I need to get to my desk."

The man unlocked the door, then locked it again behind Ned, and then went down the corridor turning on lights so Ned could see where he was going. And why not—he was being kind to one of the people who helped him put food on his table. Or so he had every reason to think.

Ned sat down at the computer of one of the partners and turned it on. While it was starting up, he installed a flash drive into the USB port of the computer. There was a Post-it note stuck to the display, with the secretary's username and password (a not uncommon practice in some offices). In less than five minutes, Ned had downloaded every spreadsheet and document file stored on the workstation and from the partner's network directory and was on his way home.

Incidentally, some companies will go to unbelievable extremes to have access to trash from a specific office. In one case, a competitor tried to bribe the cleaning crew of a medium-sized building, but was rebuffed. Then he tried to underbid the cleaning service but the owners were happy with the present crew and refused to change. He then bought the entire building, fired the janitorial crew, put in his own crew, got what he needed, and then sold the building for a lower price. "I gained a lot more that I lost," he says with a smirk.

IS PRETEXTING AGAINST THE LAW?

According to the Federal Trade Commission, the answer is yes. They define pretexting as using false information in order to get private information such as credit card numbers, Social Security numbers, and banking and telephone records. However, not all pretexting is against the law. Author Christopher Hadnagy, in his book *Social Engineering*, writes:.

> Pretexting is also used in areas of life other than social engineering. Sales; public speaking; so-called fortune tellers, neurolinguistic programming (NLP) experts; and even doctors, lawyers, therapists, and the like all have to use a form of pretexting. They all have to create a scenario where people are comfortable with releasing information they normally would not.

In the example above, and those to follow, look for the principles involved in order to protect yourself from such attacks. The case of Ned Racine, for instance, may alert you to dangers you yourself may face, even though you do not have an office away from home. If you suspect that someone is after you for whatever reason, you'll need to warn your kids, or the cleaning lady, or whoever else might be home while you are away, to never to answer the telephone, and to never to answer the door. (*Reason:* Pretexters are skilled in conning others to let them into a building and/or to give up confidential information.)

HACKING VS. SOCIAL NETWORKING

PIs, skip tracers, and bounty hunters often have more success with social networking than they do with hacking. Kevin Mitnick, in his best-seller *Ghost in the Wires*, tells how he once took some temporary work serving subpoenas. One job was to serve a subpoena on a target who lived in Las Vegas, but was in hiding. All Mitnick had to go on was the man's last known phone number.

> I called the number, an elderly lady answered, and I asked if the man was there. She said he wasn't.
>
> I told her, "I owe him some money. I can pay half now and half next week. But I'm leaving town, so I need you to call him and find out where he wants to meet me so I can pay the first half." And I said I'd call back in half an hour.
>
> After about ten minutes, I called the Switching Control Center at Centel, the local phone company. Posing as an internal employee, I had DMS-100 switch tech to do a QCM (Query Call Memory command) on the lady's number.
>
> She had made her most recent call about five minutes earlier, to a Motel 6 near the airport. I called and when I was connected to his room, I said I was from the front desk, and did he still want the roll-away bed he had asked about. Of course he said he hadn't asked about a roll-away. I said, "Is this room 106?"
>
> Sounding annoyed, he said, "No, it's 212." I apologized. My grandmother was kind enough to drive me over there.
>
> My knock was answered by "Yeah."
>
> "Housekeeping, have you a minute?"
>
> He opened the door. I said, "Are you Mr.—?"
>
> "Yeah."
>
> I handed him the documents and said, "You are served. Have a nice day."

The weak link? The elderly lady fell for a fake story and called Mitnick's target.

OBTAINING INFORMATION VIA FACEBOOK

According to Frank Ahearn, author of *How to Disappear*, the first thing a skip tracer will do when he's on your trail is to tap into your network of friends. And if you are on Facebook (even if it's set to private), your page will be a gold mine.

> Keep in mind that unless you've changed your privacy prefer-
> ences to the strictest settings, strangers will be able to see your
> friends list, even if they haven't "friended" you. Oh, but you
> can only see a handful of friends, you say. Right, but if you keep
> hitting "Reload," that handful will change every time. My col-
> leagues and I have found so many of our targets' family mem-
> bers and coworkers that way that we have a special name for it:
> The Facebook Refresh.

Once the skip tracer has the names, he'll start sending e-mails and making calls until someone sooner or later is tricked into giving information.

WATCH OUT FOR THE FLASH DRIVE TRICK

In one case, a hacker was determined to get access to a certain company's computers. A direct attack had failed to work,
so he decided to go with Plan B. First, he prepared two USB
flash drives with malicious payloads in them. Then, using a
ruse with a secretary, he gained access to one of the company's
bathrooms, where he entered a stall. He removed an envelope
from his pocket marked PRIVATE, inserted one of the flash
drives, sealed the envelope, and left it on the floor. On the way
out, he dropped the other device in the hallway near a break
room.

Out of curiosity, one of the employees did insert one of the
flash drives in a company computer, at which point the hacker
had complete access to all the company's secrets. This trick has
become fairly common but it still works, as indicated by this June
11, 2011, article on the Government Computer News Web site
(www.gcn.com)

A recent penetration test by the Homeland Security Department highlighted a glaring weakness that keeps security professionals up at night. DHS staff deliberately dropped data disks and USB flash drives in federal agency and contractor parking lots.

According to Idappcom, a network security firm, 60 percent of those planted data devices, which could easily hold malicious code, were inserted into company or agency computers. And if the data device had an official logo, the "success rate" for it being inserted into an organization's network rose to 90 percent.

"There is no device known to mankind that prevents people from being idiots," said Ray Bryant, Idappcom's CEO.

SECRET SPACES, HIDDEN PLACES

Don't laugh when I tell you this, but after hiding it, be sure you can someday still *remember* wherever it was you hid the machine pistols/ammunition/jewelry and precious stones/chemical products/clippings/videos/photographs/silver dollars/gold bullion/negotiable securities/secret maps/compromising documents/forbidden books/red-hot love letters/500-euro bills/whatever.

From 1959 until Generalissimo Franco ordered Spain's laws to be changed in 1970, my companions and I were hiding small boxes in all of Spain's fifty provinces, and with the advent of legality, a plaintive cry was heard across the land: *"I can't remember all the places where I hid things!"*

NEVER HIDE CASH IN THE MASTER BEDROOM

One of the essentials in maintaining your privacy is to pay cash at the gas station, the supermarket, and when you go shopping at the mall. Further, you need a cash reserve to prepare for the day when banks may close, or you are forced to flee, or if a government agency froze your bank accounts without warning. To do this, you must keep a fair amount of cash on hand that is easily accessible and yet invisible to burglars. But where should you keep it?

There is no such thing as a burglar-proof home that cannot be entered, nor a security system that cannot be bypassed. However, the average burglar will be inside your home for less than ten minutes. Your goal, therefore, is to keep your cash hidden for more than that length of time.

The burglar will head straight for your master bedroom. He'll check your underwear drawer, then your other drawers, and he'll look under your mattress. If he can find some cash in any of these places, he may just grab that and run. If you can afford it, therefore, leave a few hundred dollars under the mattress. Otherwise, the burglar will next check your refrigerator and your freezer so don't keep any "cold" cash in either place.

Instead, if you have a file cabinet, use one or more of the file folders for holding the cash. Title them with dull names such as "Old Tax Receipts" or "Travel Brochures." Or, if you have a library, use a box cutter to cut the center out of some book you no longer want. (Outdated computer books or AAA travel books are ideal for this.) Put your money inside and then mix the book with others in your bookcase. My favorite method, however, is to use one or more "can safes" that are available on the Internet. One of our friends from the Canary Islands keeps half a dozen such cans. She scatters them under her sink, in her pantry, and among a box of bug-spray cans in her garage.

WHERE TO HIDE OTHER ITEMS OF VARIOUS SIZES

Sadly, burglars are not the only ones to worry about. Add to the list Level Three PIs, local police, U.S. marshals, and special agents of the Drug Enforcement Administration (DEA), or the Bureau of Alcohol, Tobacco, and Firearms (ATF).

Here are a few suggestions for hiding small items in your home and yard:

- Inside hollow doors.
- In water hoses.
- Inside fuse boxes.
- In doghouses.
- Under attic insulation.
- Inside or under a furnace.
- Under fence-post tops.
- Behind wall phones.
- Under an ironing-board cover.
- In the bottom of a dog food bag.
- Behind plumbing inspection doors.
- Inside a plastic rolling pin.
- Above acoustic tile ceilings.
- In salt and pepper shakers.
- Within a sanitary napkins box.
- Above false ceilings.
- Inside zippered cushions.
- Inside the handle of a vacuum cleaner.

In any of our various homes, it would seem to be no problem to leave cash and other valuables out in plain view. After all, the addresses are secret, and if the bad guys *can't find* the house, they can't raid it! However, I do keep valuables well hidden and so should you. Can you guess why?

If a burglar is attracted to your home, it doesn't matter what arrangements have been made for privacy because it's not *you* he's after, it's the house. On the other hand, since the burglar has (hopefully) never attended a DEA seminar, nor will he have the time for that kind of a search, many of the hiding places on the DEA list are worth considering. Here are some of the ways to hide small, medium, and large items in your home.

SMALL

Save old junk-mail envelopes and put a few $50 or $100 bills in each one. Hide the envelopes in such places as:

- Sheet music in a piano bench.
- In the box of old tax receipts in a storage unit.
- In the hollowed-out section of an out-of-date software manual
- In one of the hanging files in a file cabinet
- Rolled up and inserted into a "foot powder" spray can with a removable bottom.

When my car was stolen from the airport parking building at SeaTac, the thieves broke open the glove compartment searching, I assume, for a gun. All they found were stacks of what appeared to be junk mail, so they tossed all those envelopes on the floor and the envelopes were still there when the police recovered the car. The *police* didn't notice, *either*, that two of those so-called junk-mail envelopes each had five $50 bills in them.

When I travel, I use a slim dress belt with two sections, each of which will hold three bills folded lengthwise four times. At one time I carried six Canadian $1,000 bills, but in 2001, the Canadian government pulled them off the market. However, about that time euro notes appeared, so I switched to 500 euro notes.

As for outdoor mildew and rustproof storage, nothing beats silver and gold. I am a fan of silver rounds, but since many of my readers prefer gold, $100,000 in gold coins will fit into a coffee can with room to spare.

MEDIUM

You may have books, records, pictures, cell-phone scanners, or other items that you need to keep for now. However, you do not want them found in case you die in an accident. It may be a nuisance, but consider keeping these off the premises in private storage. (In case of death, a trusted friend, whom you've instructed beforehand, will clean out the unit and dispose of the contents.

LARGE

A three-drawer fireproof file cabinet is best stored in a secret room that will hopefully be large enough to hold one or two persons as well. A room such as this will give you added security, especially if you are the wife of a traveling man who leaves you home alone.

I pass this idea on to you as worthy of consideration when you plan your next new home. The only hesitation I'd have would be that the secret room would be common knowledge among the architect, the contractor, and the workers. Also, the building plans would be on file with the city or county. Gone are the days when pirates buried treasures in deep holes, then murdered the men who'd done the work.

SPEAKING OF BURIED TREASURE . . .

The below is from the Associated Press:

> "A worker preparing a forested site in DuPont (Washington) for a park-and-ride lot unearthed a plastic garbage can containing as much as $10,000 in coins and bills . . . Sound Transit bought the 4-acre property just weeks before the buried cash turned up," said agency spokesman Lee Somerstein. . . . "It was a

bulldozer operator . . . whose machine ripped the top off a 32-gallon Rubbermaid trash can, exposed the buried money and unearthed a mystery," Somerstein said.

As this book goes to press, no one has yet come forward to claim the money.

QUESTIONS & ANSWERS

We'd like to build a secret or "panic room" but aren't such rooms horrendously expensive? (We just saw that old movie.)

After the film with Jodie Foster came out, there was an item on CNN's Headline News about the increasing number of homes that have such rooms, with costs often running up to $75,000. Any home we ever build includes a panic room, but at a minimal cost. *You don't need steel walls if the room is invisible.* If you are short of space, even a hall closet will do. The trick is that the door must not come down to the floor level. Enclose the bottom two feet and lower the top as well. Repaint or repaper the wall. Cover the opening with a mirror or a display case.

Leave a bucket in there, some bottled water, and a sleeping bag. A .12-gauge shotgun is optional.

We plan to build a low-profile safe house in the Pacific Northwest, with hidden spaces, a secret room, and perhaps even an escape tunnel. Can you help?

Schedule a consultation with me, and we'll go over the plans. I can show you an "invisible" safe house that has all of those features and more. You can take notes and copy the ideas you like. Better yet, bring $795,000, with you, and you can buy the LLC that owns it.

HOW TO SECRETLY RUN
A HOME-BASED BUSINESS

"Are You Zoned for Business?" That was the title of an article in *Home Office Computing*. The subtitle was *Registering Your Home Office Is a Difficult but Necessary Evil.*

In chapter 1, you may recall that I said, "If I mention any procedure, which I suspect might be construed as illegal in some states, provinces, or countries, I will warn you of that fact beforehand." When it comes to working at home without registering for a business license, consider yourself warned.

However, the authorities seldom if ever send out patrols to search for violators. Rather, they depend upon tips from your competitors or complaints from the neighbors. Further, the usual result of a complaint is merely a warning, so stay cool and keep these tips in mind:

- Never, ever tell your neighbors about your business.
- Do not have your customers or clients come to your home.
- Never receive deliveries at home—but then, you already

knew that. The best invisible business is run online. Payments can be either online or money orders received in the mail. No one will know your age, race, background, or if you're a first cousin to the Roswell aliens.

You can sell such a business to someone else in any state or—in some cases—any nation in the world. In 1989, one of my clients started a mail-order business from the spare bedroom in his cheap tract house in a small town in Nevada. The initial investment was $1,500. The product had to do with a paralegal service that was attractive to Europeans. The first year all he did was break even, so he lived on his savings. Then sales began to grow by word of mouth. In 1992, he withdrew a six-figure bonus (using a convoluted tax-free transaction) and kept working. In 1994, a privacy-oriented entrepreneur from Nebraska purchased 100 percent of the stock in the corporation that owned the customer list for $500,000.

Not a single neighbor knew a business had been run from that home, much less that he had been netting up to $20,000 a month before taxes. And the taxes weren't all that much—90 percent of the stock was in a charitable remainder trust, not subject to income tax. (A detail beyond the scope of this book.) However, the basic reason for starting the business was *privacy*. The fact that it did better than expected was a bonus.

HOW TO HIDE BOTH YOUR TRUE NAME AND YOUR SEX WHEN YOU RUN AN INTERNET BUSINESS

Susie—a longtime student of *How to Be Invisible*—runs a Web site that has to do with selling how-to-do-it information in a very niche field. She uses a man's name (I'll say John) because she believes—rightly or wrongly—that anyone interested in this field might pay her less attention if they knew she was a woman. She lists only a mailing (ghost) address and an e-mail address on her site. From time to time, she receives a request via e-mail for a phone number so that the sender can speak with John personally. If you were in this position, how would you respond to such a request?

Susie e-mails back that she ("John") does business only by snail mail and e-mail. That reply normally suffices. However, if the request involves what appears to be an emergency, she e-mails the man for his telephone number and then calls him from a Tracfone.

"John is not here today," she says, "but I can solve your problem," and of course she can, because she owns the business. But what if a caller insists upon a phone number so he can call John another day? Should that ever happen, Susie is prepared with an answer:

"Unfortunately, sir, John is completely deaf, which is why he uses only e-mail or snail mail. But he sure knows a lot about his subject, doesn't he!"

SHOULD YOU WORK "OFF THE BOOKS"?

If you mean, to avoid paying income tax, then the answer is no. I have never evaded income taxes nor have I ever recommended that course to anyone else. Why be a tax cheat when there are so many ways to make money and keep enough for yourself legally?

Some, of course, are in another country and unable to get a work permit—think of the million of Latinos in the United States, and hundreds of thousands of others who work illegally in Europe, Australia, and South Africa. I have several friends from Spain, for example who are currently in the States on student visas. They are working underground because they do not have and cannot get green cards. One of them has been making notes and plans to write an e-book about how to make money without a green card. If he does, it may be available later on at www .canaryislandspress.com.

ANONYMOUS PROFITS IN REAL ESTATE

In the current recession, you might think that a better subtitle would be "How to *Lose* Money in Real Estate," but—as usual— there are niche markets that are doing well.

Years ago I ran across an aging landlord from Chesapeake, Virginia, named Lonnie Scruggs. For the previous ten years he'd been buying old—and I do mean *old*—mobile homes for a few thousand dollars each. He then made a few repairs, dabbled on some paint, and priced that at double his cost. He then sold them by financing them himself, charging up to 18 percent annual interest. The reason this worked was because his low-income buyers had only two questions: (1) How much down? and (2) How much a month? These deals were easy to sell, because down payments were about $500, and monthly payments were less than $200. (Buyers paid rent to the mobile home park on their own.) Here's why it's so great from the standpoint of privacy:

- You purchase the mobile home for *cash*, so no one asks you for credit information.
- You title it in the name of a limited liability company.
- The renters will either pay cash each month, or make their checks out to whatever name you give them.

Scruggs has paperbacks books and Kindle e-books out on this subject. Check www.amazon.com.

INVISIBLE PROFILE

In general, the idea behind running any low-profile business is to keep your name out of the picture, so that you cannot be named in a lawsuit. You will, therefore, run the business in another name. It can be in the name of a nominee, a pen name, or in the name of a limited liability company. In fact, some persons use *two* LLCs, with the first one doing business and the second one as the sole member of the first. A totally different method is to use one or more established businesses as a "front," and I once ran across such a business in Boston. Here's some background information.

In 1974, I went to the Bombay Bazaar in Las Palmas de Gran Canaria to buy a new watch. At that time, Bulova was at the cutting edge of time-keeping technology, with their electronic Accutron model. Instead of *tick-tick-tick* from a balance movement, the Accutrons emitted a pleasing low-level hum from a tuning fork, and the sweep second hand moved around the dial with silky smoothness rather than by little jerks.

I bought the Spaceview model with a transparent dial, and it is still my constant companion. Among other things, it reminds me to "always look for a second solution." That is, even when I find a solution for whatever problem, I look for a second one as well. (Bulova failed the test—they neglected to look into quartz movements as a "second solution." Later, the Japanese, using quartz movements, ran over the Bulova folks like a steamroller.)

Some years ago, when in Dallas on business, the battery in my Accutron went dead. Thinking there was "no problem," I had a new battery installed. Unknown to me, however, Bulova's 1.35-volt mercuric oxide low-drain battery had been outlawed in the United States because of its mercury content, and jewelers were substituting a 1.5-volt battery. The result was that, two weeks later, half of the tuning fork's electronic circuit blew out while I was in a certain city on the East Coast. When I called the Bulova service department in Woodside, New York, I was stunned to learn that they refused to carry parts or repair Accutrons any longer. Their miserable excuse is that the 1.35-volt mercury-based batteries are no longer obtainable. But they are, in every country of the civilized world other than the United States.

So where am I going with all this? *I found a solution with a repairman who is I-N-V-I-S-I-B-L-E!*

I started my search by calling jewelers in the Yellow Pages that listed "Bulova" as one of the brands they sold. The first three assured me that Bulova Accutrons could no longer be repaired, but the fourth jeweler was my kind of man. If I'd drop off the watch, he'd see to it that an independent repairman would fix it, and put in a new Eveready #387 1.35-volt mercuric oxide low-drain battery (purchased in Canada).

"May I talk to the repairman, please?"

"No, he doesn't have any contact with the public."

At first I thought the jeweler was just trying to protect a commission, but further investigation proved this was not the case. Whoever the repairman was he deals only through established dealers, with all checks being made out to the jewelry store. And—listen to this!—the actual repairman has never been seen, and no one has a clue as to his name, address, or telephone number.

The only contact between the stores and the repairman is a courier known as Tony. Every Friday, Tony, who appeared to be in his late seventies and walked with a limp, made the rounds in the city, picking up and delivering Bulova Accutrons and similar models, receiving payment *in cash*. The storeowners were happy, because they got a commission and rendered a needed service to their customers, and we Bulova Accutron owners were happy to keep our watches running. Could this repair guy be tracked down? Without a subpoena, some industrial-strength threats, or a PI who successfully trails Tony, I don't think so. And who would want to? Why would anyone care?

Suppose, then, that you wish to set up an invisible, untraceable business, and for whatever reason do not want to use a corporation, an LLC, nor a nominee. Okay, why not copy the Bulova repairman?

1. Locate retail businesses or public offices where the owners are willing to act on your behalf in return for a commission. Contact them in person or via a representative. Your business could be in repair, replacement, software, small products, information, reports, or any other kind of business where *the customer would contact the store or office.*

2. Checks will be made out to your dealers, and the dealers will pay you or your rep in cash. They will want a receipt for their tax records, but this can be in any business name you like. Who cares; who would ever check?

3. You keep good records with QuickBooks (no audit trail when you correct errors), list the income on your personal tax return (Schedule C), and all's well with your world.

THE DANGERS OF
FACIAL RECOGNITION

"Facebook's Privacy Issues Are Even Deeper Than We Knew" was the headline at Forbes.com, just after the Black Hat Conference at Caesar's Palace in Las Vegas in August 2011. A research team at Carnegie Mellon University had showed that Facebook had become a worldwide photo identification database.

> Paired with related research, we're looking at the prospect where good, bad, and ugly actors will be able to identify a face in a crowd and know sensitive personal information about that person.

It turns out that CMU searchers didn't even have to log into Facebook to get to the photos there. They relied on just Facebook's public profile information and off-the-shelf facial recognition software, then accessed profile information through Facebook's search engine APIs. Nevertheless, they matched Facebook users with their pictures on otherwise anonymous Match .com accounts.

Drawing upon previous research, they were also relatively successful at guessing individuals' Social Security numbers. From there, of course, it is just an automated click to your Google profile, LinkedIn work history, credit report, and many other slices of private information.

Two months later, the following headline appeared on Nextgov's Web site (www.nextgov.com):

FBI TO LAUNCH NATIONWIDE
FACIAL RECOGNITION SERVICE

The article went on to state:

The FBI by mid-January [2012] will activate a nationwide facial recognition service in select states that will allow local police to identify unknown subjects in photos, bureau officials told Nextgov. . . .

Using the new Next-Generation Identification system that is under development, law enforcement analysts will be able to upload a photo of an unknown person; choose a desired number of results from two to 50 mug shots; and, within 15 minutes, receive identified mugs to inspect for potential matches. . . .

The planned addition of facial searches worries Sunita Patel, a staff attorney with the Center for Constitutional Rights, who said, "Any database of personal identity information is bound to have mistakes. And with the most personal immutable traits like our facial features and fingerprints, the public can't afford a mistake."

The article goes on to say that large-scale searches may generate a lot of false positives. Hmmm . . . might that happen with *your* picture, taken from your passport, a travel visa, any government ID, your driver's license, your or someone else's Web site, a dating site, or from Facebook (posted by you and/or your "friends")?

THE NEXT STEP IN FACIAL RECOGNITION

The next step is the face-scanning glasses that the Brazilian police plan to wear at the 2014 World Cup. A small camera fitted to their glasses will be able to capture 400 facial images per second and send them to a central computer database storing up to 13 million faces. The system can compare biometric data at 46,000 points on a face and will immediately signal any matches to known criminals or people wanted by police.

In the future, this sort of thing won't be limited to the police. Facebook has the largest collection of identified photographs in the world outside of a government, and they are currently at work on a major photo-tagging project.

HOW YOU COULD BE FALSELY TARGETED

Natick resident John Gass, who hadn't had a traffic ticket in years, was astonished when he received a letter from the Massachusetts Registry of Motor Vehicles informing him to stop driving. His driver's license had been revoked! According to the Web site www.boston.com (July 2011):

> "I was shocked," Gass said in a recent interview. "As far as I was concerned, I had done nothing wrong." After frantic calls and a hearing with Registry officials, Gass learned the problem: An antiterrorism computerized facial recognition system that scans a database of millions of state driver's license images had picked his as a possible fraud. It turned out Gass was flagged because he looks like another driver . . . and apparently, he has company. Last year, the facial recognition system picked out more than 1,000 cases that resulted in State Police investigations, officials say. And some of those people are guilty of nothing more than looking like someone else.

DOES YOUR DRIVER'S LICENSE MATCH
THE STATE WHERE YOU LIVE?

After reading previous editions of this book, some of you moved to a new state, but kept your driver's licenses from the old state. No one other than a cop or a car rental agent would of course know this, because you've been using only your passports when an ID was required.

However, what if a search of photos brings up your driver's license? It will show that you are licensed in a state different from where you actually live. (This is not likely to happen, but it *is* possible.)

CAN FACIAL RECOGNITION BE DEFEATED?

Perhaps, but only with extreme effort. Facial recognition works by measuring the distance from your eyes to another point on your face, such as your hairline, the bottom of your chin, your cheekbones, or the edge of your mouth. This is more difficult if you:

- Wear a baseball cap.
- Wear tinted or dark glasses.
- Have facial hair.
- Have on dark eyeliner.
- Wear a ski mask (you wish!).
- Smile.

A *smile?* Yes, because a smile in a picture will distort the biometrics. Now you know why the clerk at the DMV tells you not to smile for the driver's license photo. Smile anyway, and say, "I just can't help it, I'm so happy to get my license renewed."

If you are determined to post a picture of yourself anywhere

on the Internet, you might consider a picture showing your profile, thus hiding your key measurements. Or, use a photograph
where your head is just a small part of the picture, such as my
own picture on the dust jacket of this book. The lack of definition will make precise measurements difficult.

Before you allow any of your friends to take a picture of you,
hand them a card such as the one below.

If you post my picture

on the Internet . . .

YOU WILL DIE

TEN ADDITIONAL PRIVACY TIPS

Most of the following information, in no particular order, comes from my privacy blog (http://blog.invisible-privacy.com), where I have been posting tips since 2008. By the time you read this, there will be dozens if not hundreds of additional tips, so be sure to check it out.

1. HOW YOU CAN HIDE YOUR IDENTITY
WHEN YOU STAY AT A HOTEL

Suppose it is known that you will be in a big city on a certain date, and that you often stick with a certain hotel chain? How would you like to hide your identity and thus avoid calls from persons such as ex-employees, ex-wives, ex-in-laws, or even private investigators?

In days gone by, you could hide your identity by checking into a hotel under any name you liked, pay cash, and that was it. No longer, of course. All major (and most minor) hotels will not rent you a room without a valid credit card and government-issued ID. So, can you still hide your identity today? Yes, you can.

Since I am a privacy consultant, many readers of *How to Be Invisible* know that I often meet my clients at the Westin in Bellevue, the Encore in Vegas, or the W in San Francisco. Does anyone ever try to call me there?

Perhaps, but I have no way of knowing because callers will be told, "Mr. Luna is not registered here." How can this be?

Like a magician who reveals a magic trick, when I reveal my secret, it will seem to be obvious. Nevertheless, only a few of my clients who've had personal consultations with me bother to use this system. The following is how I hide my identity when staying at a hotel:

I have a single Visa credit card account, originally issued in my own name. However, I later applied for a second card on the same account. *Reason:* I needed to separate expenses when I traveled in my "professional" name. The second card was issued with no problem. You can do the same. Your reason can be that you use another name as an author, an actor, a musician, or whatever. No one will check.

Then, when you travel, you have a choice. Either travel under your real name, but give out the professional name, or vice versa. When checking in, you will be asked for ID. Show your passport. Even when you've made your reservation under the assumed name, my experience has been that all the clerk wants to see is your picture. If a question should ever arise, just explain that the name in your passport identifies you, but the reservation was made in your professional name because your credit card is in that name.

2. HOW YOU CAN HIDE YOUR SECRET
HOME ADDRESS FROM THE UPS

As has already been explained, you should never receive anything at your true home address. However, some companies irritatingly refuse to ship to a PO box. One solution might be to use the address of a relative or friend. However, that may present a serious loss of privacy. The following is a recent example of how that can be solved without using someone else's address:

Burnett Williams, recently retired, sold his home where he had lived for thirty years and moved from Montana to a secret address in Arizona. Given the way the Federal Reserve is currently printing money by the trainload, he feared that a serious devaluation was coming within a few years, so what to do with all the cash?

After checking with some knowledgeable friends, he decided to put 20 percent of it into silver bullion. The immediate problem he faced was that silver bullion is heavy and is usually shipped only by UPS. UPS keeps an international database with the address of every shipper and every receiver. Once your address gets into their system, it never gets out.

Williams was not about to let any neighbor or friend accept this shipment on his behalf because the contents (given the shipper's business name and the weight) would be obvious. End of privacy! He therefore gave the following name and address to the supplier. (This is the address of a UPS Customer Center. Note that he did not give them his distinctive first name.)

B. Williams
ATTENTION—HOLD
1975 E. Wildermuth
Tempe, AZ 85281

When he picked up the shipment he used his passport for ID, since passports never include an address. And if anyone googles "B. Williams," some 600,000 results will show up!

3. HOW TO HIDE YOUR LAST NAME
WHEN YOU ORDER ONLINE

The trick here is open a bank account in the name of a trust. Once that's done, you're all set because your credit card will have an added abbreviation after your last name. For example, let's say your name is Susan Wellington. Your credit card will read Susan Wellington TTEE. The TTEE is short for trustee and is listed because you are the trustee for your trust account.

AMAZON.COM

Open your account in the name of Susan Ttee. Forever after, Amazon will think that Ttee is your last name.

FEDEX AND UPS

Your goal is to have your books, handgun, gold bullion, or whatever, delivered to a customer service center. You order your shipment in the name of Susan W. Ttee. When you go by to pick up your package, show your passport when asked for ID. You may or may not be questioned about this, but if asked, show your credit card. A simple explanation might be: "I ordered this online and I had to fill out my name as shown on my credit card. I guess they didn't understand that Ttee just means that I am a trustee on this account but anyway, the package is for me. My name is Susan and my last name does start with a W."

4. HOW TO AVOID TROUBLE FROM TRASH TRUCK DRIVERS

The following information came from one of my readers:

> I know of one city that pays the trash truck drivers a cash bonus every time they report someone who is building or remodeling

without a permit. If the drivers see any activity, they report the address to the permit office. If no permit has been issued for that address, the building inspector makes a visit. The trash truck drivers go to every house & business in the county once or twice a week, and any construction activity is easily noticed. Even swapping out an electric water heater, a very easy job, will get you busted if you toss the box & packaging out to the curb to be picked up.

I don't know how many cities pay cash bonuses to the trash drivers but I suspect they are encouraged to report *any* suspicious activity to Homeland Security. Also, what if a burglar is paying a trash driver to watch for empty cartons from computers, flatscreen TVs, and home theater systems? The burglar can then target those homes for a visit!

Most of the trash truck drivers, of course, are just out to do their job and deserve our respect. Nevertheless, I suggest you keep a low profile by disposing of telltale boxes at some other location.

5. HOW TO ACTIVATE A NEW CREDIT CARD WITHOUT REVEALING YOUR E-MAIL ADDRESS OR TELEPHONE NUMBER

My wife has a Visa credit card in her initials and maiden name. All the bank has is an untraceable PO box in another town. No e-mail address. No telephone number. However, each time a new credit card arrives, this message is pasted across the front:

IMPORTANT
You MUST activate your card NOW to begin using your card. CALL 1-866-537-8424 from your home phone.

Why do they insist she call from our home phone? To capture the home phone number, of course. (There is also an option to activate the card by going to the bank's Web site, but this would involve giving them her e-mail address and revealing her IP address—both a no-no.) So what's a person to do?

Why, call from some other phone, of course. But do not use the telephone of any friend or relative because you do not want Wells Fargo to think you live there, either, right? One way is to use a pay phone, although pay phones are getting increasingly hard to find. Another might be to call from a library. However, we prefer to wait until our next trip. Then, we call the number from our hotel room, and, thus, the card is activated.

6. HOW TO USE A LEGITIMATE RETURN ADDRESS THAT WILL NOT BE TRACED BACK TO YOU

In the UK, it is a common practice to mail letters with no return address. Nevertheless, I do not recommend it and here's why:

Suppose you made an error in the address, or the person you sent the letter to has changed to a PO box, or perhaps has moved away? Your letter will then go to the dead-letter office where it will eventually be opened. Will your address be inside? Or even a check? Further, you may assume the letter was received, whereas actually, it was not. Many of you readers may already have a ghost address in another state or a foreign country. If so, why not use that address as your return address on some of your mail? That way, if a letter bounces, you will get it back from your mail-forwarding service.

7. HOW TO DELAY THE SERVING OF A SUBPOENA

A subpoena is an order, usually signed by a notary public, to attend a legal proceeding such as a trial or deposition. A subpoena *duces tecum* means you are ordered to bring certain documents with you, which can be anything from bank statements to old love letters. The purpose of a subpoena is to force you to produce something you do not want to produce, and/or to appear in a civil or criminal court case when that is on the very bottom of your "things-I'd-like-to-do" list. Although it is not correct to say that if they can't find you they can't serve you, this process certainly can, and often should be, delayed as long as possible, thus giving you time to think things out.

(At this late date, don't do a Nixon and erase tapes, nor an Ollie North and shred documents. If your tape, document, or photo files need work, stop reading *now* and start erasing, burning, flushing, burying, encrypting, and shredding *before* the storm clouds gather.)

In a civil case, a subpoena can be delivered by a law firm employee, a professional process server, peace officer, or anyone else of legal age (in some counties, registered and bonded) capable of making multiple attempts, able to correctly fill out the proof or certificate of service, and who can testify as a credible witness if the service is challenged.

In a criminal case, service will be achieved if you acknowledge receipt of the subpoena by telephone or mail, as well as in person. *It has even been done to those who have Facebook!* The way you identify yourself (should you ever want to . . .) is by name, date of birth, and driver's license number.

Delaying service of a subpoena is not for amateurs. Beyond a certain point, if it can be shown that you *willfully* disobeyed it, the court can issue a bench warrant for your arrest. Now is the time to call in an experienced shark—preferably of the species great white, bull, tiger, or oceanic whitetip. This lawyer will know many sneaky tricks about *serving* subpoenas and will, thus, be able to tell you how and up to what point you can delay service.

Now then, if service appears to be inevitable, at least take control of *where* and *when* this is to happen. Don't get caught unaware like Franklin K. from Cleveland. He owed his lawyer

money, but he had a daughter's wedding coming up, so he chose
to stall the lawyer and throw an elaborate wedding reception.
The lawyer learned about this and decided to cause the most
possible humiliation to his delinquent client.

At the precise moment Franklin stood up to propose a toast to
the new bride and groom, the sheriff barged in and served Franklin
with a subpoena! Learn from this, and if you fear you will be
served with a subpoena, do not attend a public gathering where
you may be known, and do not admit your identity to a stranger.

If you *are* served, have your legal beagle bring a motion to
quash. (You may have heard that the process server must touch
your face or body with the papers. Not true; he can just toss the
papers at your feet, or whatever.) Have him claim that service
was improper and statutory requirements were not met.

When all else fails, follow the advice of the anonymous writer
who penned these words:

> *When uncertain,*
> *Or in doubt,*
> *Run in circles!*
> *Scream and shout!*

8. HOW TO HANDLE UNWANTED MAIL

Make up some stickers with either of these two messages:

- MOVED. NO FORWARDING ADDRESS
- NOT DELIVERABLE AS ADDRESSED
  UNABLE TO FORWARD

When an unwanted letter arrives, place the sticker over the
address (but not the name). You must also black out the barcode
along the bottom. Then, draw an arrow pointing back to the return address.

9. HOW TO SEND PRIVATE,
SECRET INFORMATION BY E-MAIL

- Go to *www.thismessagewillselfdestruct.com*
- Enter a message in the box on the left.
- Enter a password. (This is an option, but is recommended. It can be something simple, such as the first name of the recipient or the number of a PO box, or the day of the week. Send a clue about this password to the recipient in advance.)
- Check the box where you accept the Terms of Service.
- Click on the button "Save This Message."
- A URL will then show up. Click on the small icon at the end of the URL. It will say "COPY."
- Address an e-mail to yourself first, to test this out. In the body, hit "Control+C" to paste the URL in the message. Send it.
- When the e-mail arrives, click on the URL.
- Enter the password.
- Read your test message. Remember, once you leave the page, the message is *gone*.

10. HOW TO CREATE AN INVISIBLE OWNER
FOR YOUR NEW BUSINESS

The "owner" will be invisible because he or she *does not exist*. Unless fraud is involved, I believe this practice to be entirely legal. Let's suppose your name is Anita B. Chavez, Golda A. Goldstein, or Bashiyra Binte Nur Um Lifti. You resolve to start a business via the Internet, and you decide that, in the particular field you have chosen, a generic-sounding man's name would look better.

First, choose a three-word business name with the same

initials as yours. Then invent a man's name with the same initials. For example:

Your actual name:	Anita B. Chavez
Business name:	Awesome Birthday Cards
"Owner" name:	Albert B. Caldwell
Checks made out to:	A.B.C. (bank will allow this)

The opposite is true, of course, if you are a man who wishes to sell merchandise that will appeal to women. Choose a woman's name that seems best to go with the product.

HOW TO DISAPPEAR AND NEVER BE FOUND

The best time to prepare an escape is before the trouble starts. And what might this trouble be? It could be anything from a PI or an impending court case to some personal enemy who's sworn to kill you. So then, while the skies are still sunny and there's peace in the valley, prepare for the time when you might have to flee. The following are your three top priorities:

1. Have a detailed plan.
2. Have a valid passport.
3. Have cash on hand.

There are varying levels of disappearances. Let's start with the most common one.

LEVEL ONE ESCAPE

This is most often used when a threat comes suddenly and without warning, just as lightning may strike from a clear blue sky.

Often one must flee within twenty-four hours, and sometimes in twenty-four minutes.

Let's say you are a young woman who's just learned that your ex-lover is on the way to your city, and he's carrying handcuffs and duct tape. He has illegal access to records normally confined to the police and the government so the time to run is *now*! Remove the battery from your cell phone or else wrap it tightly in aluminum foil. Empty your bank account and/or borrow from your friends. From this point on, do not use a credit or a debit card. Make no further withdrawals from an ATM.

Gas up the car and flee the city and if possible the state. Obey all traffic signs and stay within the speed limit. Despite the fact your ex-lover has a friend in law enforcement, it is extremely unlikely that the friend would dare put out an all-points bulletin (or BOLO, which stands for "be on the lookout"), because it could cost him his job.

From this point on, use only the U.S. mail to communicate with your family and friends. Avoid all major hotel and motel chains because they demand ID and enter it in their computer databases. Instead, choose a small mom-and-pop motel where they will accept whatever name you give them as long as you pay cash. Or, better yet, stay with an old friend who is unknown to your stalker, or rent a room from a private party, using another name. (Use your "new" name.) Then use a pay phone to call someone back home who can tell you what's going on. Only when the coast is clear will you return.

LEVEL TWO ESCAPE

This is when you need to vanish for a few years, perhaps until some certain time period has run out. If you can afford to do so, get out of the country. One of my readers had to make a run in 2008. He fled to Thailand and has been happy there. However, that's a long and expensive trip. My own preference would be Mexico.

Take a bus or (preferably) fly to Guadalajara, Jalisco, then catch a taxi or a bus up to the Lake Chapala area. Stay for a few days at a bed-and-breakfast in Chapala or Ajijic, then look for a condo. You can rent a two-bedroom condo in a gated community for about $35 a day or $750 for a month, no questions asked.

Why Lake Chapala? One reason is the climate—one of the world's best. Another is that violent crime is low in that area. English is spoken in most business places, unlike some other parts of Mexico. Best of all, *you'll not stand out*, because you'll be among thousands of Americans and Canadians who live all along the north shore of the lake.

LEVEL THREE ESCAPE

This is when you plan to cut all ties and apparently vanish from the face of the earth. It is extremely difficult, often impossible, and resorted to only when all other options have been exhausted. Before you go, pick up a copy of Frank Ahearn's book *How to Disappear*, which deals primarily with extreme situations.

Even Frank, however, has this to say about a permanent disappearance: ". . . you can no longer just pick up the phone and call your family. You'll lose touch with a lot of people you care about. You're going to get lonely."

If you can afford it, leave the country. Don't try to hide in Western Europe or in any police state. A good choice might be one of the tax havens in order to minimize any requirements for filing a tax form. A court name change and new identity documents from another country will enable you to stay out of the international databases at airports, seaports, train stations, etc.

However, no matter how much money you have, or in what part of the earth you live, if someone with unlimited funds (such as a government) is after you, you will sooner or later be caught. This is because all it takes is one single mistake to blow your cover. Often this is because you send an e-mail, a letter, or make a call to a friend, relative, or associate. As far as sneaking back to your home country for a quick visit, you may as well plan to be caught.

LEAVE THE KIDS BEHIND

This is a tough decision, but you have to think of what's best for the children. Once the authorities know children are involved, they will be highly motivated to bring you down (think *Amber Alert!* and pictures on the nightly TV news). This is especially the case if you are a man, because you may be accused of child abuse.

In any case, whether you're a man or a woman, trying to escape from a criminally abusive person is fraught with danger. For that reason, document the abuses well beforehand and then flee to a shelter with your children. Once there, make sure that a service worker gets whatever documentation you have, before you move on. The fact that you took yourself to a children's shelter or to a battered-woman's shelter will help establish your innocence in any allegations that surface later.

SLOW DOWN ANY PURSUIT

Before you run from an abusive ex-husband or ex-wife, plan your escape in advance. Confiscate any firearms they may have and get rid of them. Clean out your bank accounts, scoop up anything small that you can later sell on Craigslist or use to get a loan at a pawn shop. Disable your ex's vehicle, but not by setting it on fire or crashing it somewhere. Do something that will not be obvious, such as pouring long-grain rice into the radiator.

Be sure not to do that in a garage, however, as the green fluid will slop out on the floor and give away the plan. So if that won't work, then take off the oil filler cap and pour in as much sand as you can. (Don't bother with sugar in the gas tank, however. That's been debunked on Snopes, *MythBusters*, and Tom and Ray's *Car Talk*.)

On the other hand, if giving away your flight does not matter, then just cut every cable you can find under the hood. Or, drop a wrench across the battery terminals and jump back. Or, remove the valve caps to flatten all four tires. Or if you're *really* mad, all of the above.

QUESTIONS & ANSWERS

We are about to move to another state. Is it safe to use a mover such as Allied, Bekins, or Mayflower?

Not if you value your privacy. Most—if not all—interstate moving services keep computer records and PIs know and use this. Keep in mind that even though you give the movers a different name, the computers can be searched by address as well. If, therefore, an investigator tracks down your present address and discovers you have moved, he will have an accomplice check the records to see what name you used, and the destination street address.

When we move, I pay a driver to rent a Penske rental truck in his name. I then look under "Movers" in the Yellow Pages. There is usually a subsection called "Student Movers," self-employed husky young men that load and unload trucks for an hourly wage. They load the truck, the driver drives it, and at the destination another set of student movers unload it. My driver then either drops off the truck in a nearby city, or drives it back to the city of origin. Penske, as well as other major truck rental companies, puts everything into their computers, but what do they have? Certainly not my name, and thus not my previous street address nor the new one. Incidentally, you will often save a bundle of money with this method.

How might a PI locate my home address despite taking all precautions?

Here's the PI's challenge—let's call him Oscar. All Oscar has, so far, is your name (let's say it's John Aemisegger), your religion (Mormon), the cell phone number you used just once to call a toll-free number, an e-mail address picked up when you contacted a known associate, and a strong suspicion that you live in the Seattle, Washington, area. Oh—and that as a hobby you collect prewar Martin guitars. The PI's goal is to turn over your true home address to his multimillionaire client in Chicago. Oscar doesn't know the purpose of this search, and doesn't care. The money is good.

You have just moved with your wife and children from your former home in Dallas to the Seattle suburb of Medina. You've used an untraceable nominee to rent your home, connect the utilities, sign up for the Internet with CLEAR (using a ghost address), and open bank accounts with Columbia and HomeStreet Banks.

Your cell phone Since the PI has your cell phone number, all he has to do is have a confederate in the wireless service provider ping your phone at night. This will reveal your location.

Your best protection will be to dump your present cell phone and either pick up a Tracfone, or have a nominee get you a smartphone in his name. This new number you should give out only to trusted associates and family members. Either that or always remove the battery or wrap your smartphone in aluminum foil before you take it home.

Your kids' school There's no chance of privacy in the public school system. All Oscar has to do is bribe someone in the

Seattle area schools to get the home addresses for any students named Aemisegger. There are only two remedies for this danger. Either homeschool your kids or put them in a private school willing to guarantee their privacy.

Your religion   This takes a number of calls to Salt Lake City, Utah, but eventually Oscar contacts a fellow PI who is a member of the Latter-day Saints (LDS). Joey spins an intricate story about how he wants to surprise his old friend John Aemisegger by showing up at whatever meetinghouse he attends. Once he knows the address, he will show up on Sunday, ask someone to point you out, and then follow you home.

To avoid this scenario, at the very least, attend a ward in a nearby suburb and under no condition reveal your true home address.

> *News flash February 2012*: I just now heard from our old friends Ben and Ivy, who had been living and working in Baja California Sur, Mexico. Six months ago, Ben stopped at a stop sign in Cabo San Lucas when a small truck careened around the corner and struck Ben's SUV. The driver was ejected and the truck landed on top of the driver, killing him instantly. Ben was heartbroken, but the police cleared him (after photographing him and taking his prints) since the accident was through no fault of his own. Nevertheless, Ben and Ivy moved up to Jocotepec, Jalisco, to start a new business and dim the memories of the tragic accident in Cabo.
>
> Then, on a Sunday just eight days ago, two brothers of the dead truck driver showed up at the *Iglesia de Jocotepec*, flashing a copy of the photo of Ben that had been taken by the police, and asking if anyone knew him! Without going into details, Ben and Ivy have already moved to a small village in southern Mexico. Other than me (they know I can keep a secret), they have told no one their new

address. Not their friends, not their siblings, and not even their parents.

"Ivy and I never in our wildest dreams," says Ben, referring to the accident, "imagined that in just one split second our lives could be so drastically changed!"

Do you suppose that something similar could some day happen to *you*?

Your hobby   Oscar loves targets who have a hobby. In this case he pulls up a picture of a prewar Martin guitar and puts an ad on the Seattle Craigslist:

> **"Emergency financial disaster forces me to sell my
> grandfather's 1940 Martin D-45.
> Serious inquiries only.
> Will sell for 85% of appraisal if sold within five days.
> Terms, cash.
> Will meet only at a public location such as the parking
> area of a bank.**

Three days later, you answer the ad, using the name Raymond. A meeting is set up at the parking lot of a Key Bank in Bellevue. Oscar says he'll be driving a light-blue late-model Jaguar, and what will you be driving?

"A black Lexus hybrid."

Oscar, in his usual nondescript Camry, sees your Lexus come into the parking lot. He patiently waits for you to give up and return home. When you finally do, Oscar follows you home.

This may be your greatest danger—that you or even a relative or friend coming to see you will be followed. But is it likely? No. The expense of such a campaign would be mind-boggling and the chances of a private investigator having an unlimited expense account are minimal to none.

COOL STUFF THAT DID NOT
FIT IN EARLIER

If Sherlock Holmes were alive today and on the trail of a terrorist, he would not have to leave his rented first-floor flat at 221B Baker Street, London. Instead, he would be hacking into confidential databases on his computer, making "pretext" telephone calls on his untraceable mobile phone, and squeezing information from his Muslim informants in the Arab world.

Contrast that with the average private investigator. Even other PIs lament the fact that there are so many incompetent and/or shady characters in their field.

ARE MOST PIs COMPETENT?

No more than all lawyers are competent. As in any other profession, there are a few experts, but many more who barely plod through. To illustrate, consider the famous Barbara Kurth Fagan case:

Stephen and Barbara Fagan had been married for five years, eloping to Haiti on the day that Stephen divorced Leah, his first wife. Then came a venomous divorce. He got the house. Barbara got the kids. He didn't like that, and on October 28, 1979, he snatched the children, then only two and five, from his ex-wife's home in suburban Boston. He fled with the girls to Palm Beach County, Florida, where his parents and a sister already lived. He changed the girls' names to Rachael and Lisa and his own to William Stephen Martin.

Back in Massachusetts, Barbara regained her maiden name of Kurth and filed a criminal complaint. Over the years, she hired various private investigators, but they came up blank. Finally, she gave up. She pressed ahead with her own life, remarried, and became a noted expert in cell biology.

Meanwhile, her ex-husband fashioned a good life for himself in South Florida: big houses, fast cars, and very rich wives. Nearly twenty years passed before someone in his or his latest wife's family decided Stephen's days of high living should come to an end. A tip to the authorities was all it took. Police nabbed him at his $2.2 million oceanfront estate, bought by wife number four, and he was returned to Massachusetts to face felony charges of kidnapping.

Why couldn't Barbara track him down? One reason was given in the May 25, 1998, issue of *Newsweek*:

> Fagan and his daughters insist Kurth should have been able to find them if she'd really searched. Kurth's family says she spent more than $10,000 on lawyers and private investigators— to no avail. A 1982 report from one PI warns her that staking out Fagan's sister's home in Florida would be an expensive long shot.

Others say she spent triple that but whatever it was, either it was not enough, or—more likely!—she hired the wrong investigators.

TRAVEL TIPS

PRIVATE HOME

Before you leave on a long trip, do you leave a key with a neighbor? I suggest you not only *not* leave a key, but do not even say you are leaving. (Use timers that turn on lights, TV, stereo, sprinklers, etc., at varying times.) Louis R. Mitzell Jr., in his book *Invasion of Privacy*, tells the story of a Maryland couple who, before leaving on a vacation in August 1994, left a key with a neighbor. When they returned from their trip they picked up the key, thanked the neighbor, and thought no more about it.

"Then," writes Mitzell, "in January 1995, the couple was adjusting a heating vent in their bathroom when they discovered a camera. Later that night, the couple found a second camera behind a heating vent in a dressing room and followed cables leading through their attic, down a drainpipe, and underground into their neighbor's home. The neighbor had been watching the couple in the bathroom and dressing room for months—and it wasn't against the law."

APARTMENT

The problem here is that even if you do not leave a key with anyone when going on vacation, the landlord *does* have a key. Landlords surreptitiously enter apartments more often than you might think—in fact, it once happened to me. That was fifty-six years ago, but there were such serious consequences that I haven't forgotten it yet.

Anthony Herbert, in his book *Complete Security Handbook*, has this to say in the section about locks:

> Change them without the management's knowledge. (Remove the cylinder, take it to a locksmith, and get combination changed.)

If the manager or janitor later complains, ask why he was attempting to enter your apartment while you were not present. Better to incur a minor lease violation than to be dead!

No one should be permitted to visit your apartment unaccompanied, except in a life-and-death emergency!

CHECK YOUR LAPTOP

If you travel to the UK and carry a laptop with sensitive information, beware of random checks. An agent might ask, "Do you have any pornography on your hard drive?" Even though you have no such thing on there and tell him so, he'll say, "Well then, you won't mind if we turn it on and have a look, right?" If a password is needed, he will ask for it. If a file is encrypted, he will tell you to unencrypt it. This is beginning to happen in other countries, and it may soon be coming to an airport or a border crossing near you. One remedy—if you must get a secret file through customs—is to mail it ahead on a memory chip. Another is to have everything in the cloud.

CROSSING INTO MEXICO OR CANADA

In an emergency, you may be forced to journey north or south. If so, and if you are a native-born U.S. citizen, there should normally be no problem when crossing a border in either direction, as long as neither you nor your vehicle look suspicious.

You should know, however, that there are two types of border inspections, primary and secondary. You do not want secondary, not ever, because then your name will go into the computer and, to paraphrase the ads for the Roach Motel, travelers who check *in* to the computer never check out.

Suggestions:

- Dress like a tourist. Clean and neat, but no tie.

- Do not cross with anything to declare, or with any item even remotely suspicious. No fruit, no weapons, no drugs. Best way to cross is on a tour bus. Next best way is on foot, at a busy crossing, during the busiest hours, but taking a car is certainly more convenient, despite the fact that your license plate may go into a computer. (Here's where it pays off to have your car registered in the name of an LLC.)

- Do not cross into Mexico with an RV if you can avoid it. Some Americans have been arrested in Mexico and held under false pretenses, with the goal of allowing the American to go free if he leaves his motor home behind. (An RV is okay for Canada.)

- If there are several lines leading to multiple booths at the crossing, pick your lane and then stick with it. If you change lanes, the inspector from the original lane may spot you, think you're trying to avoid him, and make you get back in line. Then, when your turn comes, you'll get more attention than you really wanted to receive.

Never cross in either direction with a flippant attitude, because both customs inspectors (CIs) and immigration inspectors (IIs) have you in their total power. They can search you, your vehicle, and your belongings for whatever reason, or for no reason at all. Therefore, before you approach the border, first check your wallet or purse, and then the glove compartment and the trunk. (If you carry my book with you, put on a different dust jacket!) Be prepared to answer any questions whatsoever, no matter how personal or insulting. Lawyers (and some egocentric businessmen) have been known to say, "Do I *have* to answer that?" The response, as given by Customs Inspector Ned Beaumont in his book *Beat the Border,* is:

You don't have to answer. But then again, you don't have to cross the border. And you're not going to cross the border until you answer that question and *any others I see fit to ask*. Understand?

CIs and IIs are skilled at deception, aka lying. If they preface something by saying, "You don't need to worry about thus-and-so . . ." *start worrying*! They may try the good cop/bad cop routine, like in the movies. Remember that it's really bad cop/worse cop. These folks are not your buddies. Keep cool and collected on the outside, skeptical and cynical on the inside. Beaumont makes this point in his "People Smarts" section:

> An inspector talks to more liars in a month than the layman does in a lifetime. How good at spotting liars do you think that inspector is going to be in a year? Or five? Or ten? I've worked with inspectors who'd been on the job for twenty years. They could detect a lie . . . *without fail*, in the first five seconds of the inspection.

When you are asked for the purpose of your trip, do not just answer "business" or "pleasure," the inspectors hear that all the time. Be specific: "We're going up to Abbotsford to buy a Clipper canoe," or "We're going to the boat show at the Winnipeg Convention Centre."

If they ask you if you have ever been arrested, *tell the truth*—even if it was a false arrest just after World War II and you only spent one night in jail. Their computers are connected with U.S. law-enforcement databases going back to the Spanish–American War! (Slight hyperbole here, but not much.)

> *A final word of warning:* Don't even *think* of using a false ID. Even if it's perfect, *you'll* know it's not, and the inspector will sense that fact.

HOW TO DEAL WITH CLERKS AND TELLERS

First of all, dress like they do, or just a bit better. No matter how convinced you are that clothes make the man or woman, reading John T. Molloy's bestseller, *Dress for Success*, will make you even more of a true believer. To Molloy's book I add the following:

If you are a woman, dress and act like a woman, emphasis on "dress" as in the noun. If you are a man, and if getting others to accept your requests for privacy is high on your list of priorities, show up freshly shaved and with a short haircut. Right or wrong, I often refuse requests from anyone who draws attention to himself or herself by outward appearance rather than by inward qualities of honesty, integrity, loyalty, and virtue. (I wish they'd teach that in grade schools.)

Next, private investigators suggest that when at all possible, *deal with the opposite sex*. This applies to trips to the bank, the county courthouse, the utility companies, and to any other location where low-level clerks deal with the public. If you are a woman, seek out a man. If you are a man, talk to a woman.

CREDIT CARD SECURITY MEASURE

Restaurants and other businesses sometimes toss out credit card receipts without shredding them. To protect yourself against this possibility, as soon as you sign the slip, *cross out the last four digits of the number* (both on the original, and on your copy). If anyone protests, assure him or her that you absolutely positively have this legal right.

However, the best protection is to never, ever, use a credit card at a restaurant, bar, saloon, massage parlor, or anywhere else where you are allowed to pay your bill in dollars, euros, pesos, rubles, pounds, yen, or rupees.

FAKE IDS

It is useless to order fake IDs on the Internet. Either you won't get anything at all, or what you do get will be worthless. Here is an additional reason: Sooner or later these companies get busted. When they do, the authorities will of course grab the customer list. Would you like them to spot *your* name and address on that list?

HERE'S A *REALLY* LOW PROFILE

Consider the methods of Kate M——, one of my readers, who takes her privacy very seriously indeed. She has found the people she meets uninterested in privacy, and skeptical about her concerns, but that hasn't stopped her. "I've mostly quit telling others about it and just quietly go about the business of protecting myself without telling anyone what I'm doing," says Kate. She's chosen to work from home for maximum flexibility and privacy, staying in control of her own schedule and managing to avoid the crowds. "Often, I go grocery-shopping late at night (eleven P.M.) or even at two or three A.M., at the store that's open twenty-four hours. Advantages include no traffic; parking right at the front door of the supermarket; no lines. . . . I can do my shopping in 30 percent less time. Plus, I see almost no one. Also, I can check my PO box and drive by my ghost address (a lockable mailbox on a rural road.) Even without tinted windows, driving at night means fewer people can recognize me. Even my nondescript old car and its color are harder to recognize at night. When I park the car out in public in the daytime, I'm now very sensitive to making sure there are no identifying items inside (letters or anything with my name on it). But I've also discovered that when I shop in the daytime, if I park in an out-of-the-way place at the outer edge of the parking lot, there are fewer people who will walk past my car on their way into the store/mall. So fewer people to notice my car."

However, I do not necessarily recommend Kate's use of the dark to enhance her privacy. In many areas, it would be dangerous for a lone woman to be out so late at night.

THE "LAST FOUR" DIGITS

Does it sound innocent enough when you are asked for "the last four digits" of your Social Security number? For example, cable TV operators ask that question when you order their service (assuming you wisely decline to read off the number of your driver's license.) This number can identify you, because who else with your same name would also have the same last four digits of the SSN? The easy solution is to have some other four-digit number ready to use. Think about it ahead of time. Perhaps it will be a date in history, or the house number where you once lived long ago.

SERIOUS WARNING ABOUT RÉSUMÉS!

A lead article in the newsletter *Bottom Line Personal*, based on an interview with me, brought this excellent advice from a reader. Writing to me as "a public service," a reader of the interview warned:

> You neglected to point out how dangerous it is to put one's résumé on the Internet. I am a professional recruiter and I can tell you more harm can come from this one action than anything else. There are malevolent people out there who are profiling everybody who has a résumé on the 'Net. It is by far the most dangerous thing you can do—it goes way beyond anything you

wrote about. Nothing you wrote even compares to the damage done by allowing so many people to see your résumé; where you live, where you have worked, your references, salaries, etc. Please let people know they must *never ever* put a résumé on the Internet. *NEVER EVER!*

FILLING OUT FORMS

A recent documentary on TV showed how private information is picked up and sold to criminals involved in identity theft. *Tens of thousands of businesses toss out application forms without shredding them.* This includes applications for employment, for loans, and for credit cards. If you have *any* family members currently filling out such forms, make sure that they never list your home address and specifically ask how such information is later disposed of.

RECORDED MUSIC ON HOLD

When some large corporations—especially the telephone companies—put you on hold with recorded music, the company operator does *not* hear the music. Instead, he or she is listening to what you may be saying to another person while waiting to come back on line.

NEVER HIRE AN EMPLOYEE

There is only one way to keep your private life private (and stay out of the dreaded New Hires list). You must work for yourself. If you are (or plan to be) a carpenter, a salesperson, an artist, an architect, an interior decorator, a hairdresser, or any similar profession where you can work alone, I suggest you do work alone. The same applies to starting your own small business. You may not get rich, but you can certainly shoot for $100,000 a year. That will be sufficient to live a simple, debt-free life.

In fact, the absolute best kinds of home-based businesses are those that can be run alone or just with help from family members. Many a small business, although successful in the beginning, has come to grief when the owner was tempted to expand. Business writer Michael LeBoeuf, in his book *The Perfect Business*, lists some of the problems connected with hiring one or more employees:

- Your freedom and flexibility will be forever restricted.
- You must give up privacy when an outsider comes into your home.
- You are now responsible for bringing in more money to cover wages and benefits.
- The government will burden you with odious payments and record-keeping chores.
- If an employee fails to show up for work, the extra work will either have to be done by you, or it won't get done at all.
- Every time someone quits, you have to start all over.

To the above, I would add one more caveat. Judging by what I read in the papers these days, if you have to fire a woman, she might come back to you with a charge of discrimination or harassment. If you fire a man, he might come back with a gun.

ARE YOU UNDER SURVEILLANCE?

In days gone by, an unfamiliar van parked across the street from your house or apartment might be a signal that a PI was inside. However, the public is getting familiar with this, so the latest

ploy is to use a generic sports utility vehicle (SUV). The tip-off
in this case may be a darkened window where the *driver* sits. In
many states it is against the law to put a dark tint on the driver
and passenger door windows. Therefore the PI carries a piece of
darkened Plexiglas, cut out in the shape of the window, and puts
it in place only when he is parked and doing surveillance work.

INFORMATION-SHARING

Airline passengers are not the only ones being secretly profiled
to determine if they are a danger to flight safety or for any other
reason. Since 9/11, the private sector has also been sharing information with the government. Many supermarkets, of course,
make this information available, but so do clubs you might not
think of, such as the National Association of Scuba Divers. Li-
braries and bookstores are under pressure as well. And especially
FedEx and UPS.

By the way, did you know that some national hotel chains
share lists of movie titles—including pornos—rented by its customers? While the name of the movie isn't on the bill, it *is* included in the customer profile. This information is shared with
their many affiliates, including other hotels and restaurants.

HOW TO COPE WITH THE LOSS OF YOUR HOME

"You may not realize it when it happens," wrote Walt Disney, "but
a kick in the teeth may be the best thing in the world for you." But
how could losing your home be good news? Let me count the
ways:

1. **Lesson learned.** Never again buy anything that you cannot
   pay cash for.

2. **Relief.** No more backbreaking mortgage payments. No more taxes, no more upkeep, no more being locked into the burden of long-term debt. All you have to pay now is rent.

3. **Freedom.** Suppose you are renting from month to month, and an obnoxious family moves in next door, or if drug dealers start dealing in your area, or if a nearby barking dog keeps you awake at night. You just move!

4. **Privacy.** If you have been getting mail and deliveries at home, or if your home address is listed in databases, or if it appears on your driver's license, your only solution will be to move—and then follow the principles outlined in this book. Although most readers can see the wisdom of this, they usually feel that selling their home and moving to another location is too great a sacrifice. But if your home is repossessed, why, here's your chance for true privacy at last!

MAGNETIC LOCKS

These locks are also marketed under various trade names. They are extremely useful for purposes of privacy. There is no keyhole to give away private hiding spaces. Suppose, for example, that you slip your laptop into such a place whenever you are away from home. If an agent secretly enters your home on a "sneak and peak" warrant, he will almost certainly not find your computer. However, if he does, he will have had to break into the space, and this means that at least you now *know* what has happened!

A $20 UNIT THAT WILL PUT ANY BURGLAR ON THE RUN!

The authority for the above statement comes from Jack MacLean, an electronics genius with an IQ of 167 and the author of *Secrets of a Superthief.* Before he went to prison, he was responsible for hundreds of burglaries that netted him $133 million worth of jewels.

MacLean interviewed 300 other burglars during his years in prison and included their answers in his amazing book. He asked them such questions as how they chose which homes to burgle, how they broke in, whether or not they cut the phone lines in advance, and what might scare them into calling off the job. The following is one of the questions in the book:

> If you had cut the phone lines of a resident you were burglarizing and at some point heard from inside that same residence, coming from the window, an extremely loud horn, what would you do?

"Ready for this?" asks MacLean. "One hundred percent said they'd be gone in a second." (The actual answers were cruder but the author preferred not to print them.)

> *Note:* To obtain an "extremely loud horn," pick up a portable air horn at any marine supply store or order it on Amazon.com. Be sure to get one that sells for about $20, because the $10 ones are not as loud.

PRIVACY PROBLEMS IN PUBLIC SCHOOLS

If you have children in a public school, have you taught them how *not* to answer questions that invade their—and often your!—privacy? Here's a typical question, taken from a Minnesota's Basic Skills Writing Test. Each student was asked the following essay question:

> Your teacher has asked you to write about one thing you would like to change about yourself. Name one thing about yourself

and give specific reasons why you would like to change it. Give enough details so your teacher will understand your ideas.

Explain to your children that their answers may become a part of their student files . . . and come back years later to haunt them.

ALLOW YOUR KIDS TO SKIP COLLEGE

Four of the five richest persons in America are college dropouts.

—*FORBES* MAGAZINE

The majority of today's high school graduates should never go to college. Often, they have no idea what they want to do, once they graduate. If you are concerned about morals, think of the peer pressure involving drugs, binge drinking, and indiscriminate sex. If you are concerned about privacy, remember that all privacy will be lost until they graduate or drop out. If you are concerned about money, remember that you or they will end up tens of thousands of dollars in debt, with no guarantee whatsoever of a high-paying job after graduation.

CONSIDERING A MOVE TO ANOTHER COUNTRY?

This past year I've been getting a lot of e-mails from readers who ask about leaving their native land. Unlike a Level Three Escape, where you're on the run, this chapter is for those of you who currently have no serious problems, but are just fed up with such things as the Patriot Act, Homeland "Security," and/or the current or incoming administration.

WHERE MIGHT YOU MOVE TO?

No easy answer to this one, folks. How much money do you have put away? Will you have to work in the new country? Do you speak the language of the new country? If not, are you willing to learn? Are you allergic to extremes in the weather? Worried about crime? Beautiful scenery a must? Good air travel connections? Do you have children and if so, what about schools? Are you sure you're familiar with *all* the laws that apply to expats?

Want to hear a horror story? One of my entrepreneurial clients I'll call Harry moved to Europe in 2005. He started up a small company, sold it, and started up a second company, which was immediately successful. Within months, hundred of thousands of euros were flowing into and out of his bank accounts. A local accountant helped Harry file U.S. tax returns, and he dutifully reported—as required by law—all of his overseas earnings. In the fall of 2011, he returned to the states and only then did it come to light that one tiny detail had been overlooked.

TDF 90-22.1

Treasury Department Form 90-22.1 must be filed every year if you have an interest in any foreign bank accounts that at any time of the year are worth $10,000 or more. This report is *separate from your income tax return*. The penalties for not filing it are brutal. Harry was faced with a total penalty of more than $800,000, and it *must* be paid.

Keeping Harry's experience in mind, I'll now mention several of my favorite places.

READ THIS FIRST

Do not be deceived when you read about living well in a foreign land on as little as $1,000 or $1,500 a month. Sometimes the prices date back to previous years, sometimes it's what the natives pay, and sometimes it just pure hyperbole.

Exception: Our good friends Chad, Gretchen, and their son, Chase, work as volunteer missionaries in a small town along the Ecuadorian coast for ten months each year. The other two months they come back to the states, working long hours in a janitorial business that allows them to save $10,000 in that short time—more than enough to return to Ecuador for another ten months because they squeak by down there on $800 a month. That even includes keeping an old Land Cruiser running.

However, the village is remote, the climate along the coast is hot and humid, and they live with the bare basics. Don't expect to imitate their lifestyle.

PERPETUAL TOURIST (PT)

If you have a fixed income, or if you can do business from anywhere via the Internet, then the most private way—by far!—is to travel abroad as a perpetual tourist. The limits of how long you can stay in a country as a tourist are often just ninety days, after which you must leave for at least ninety days, so you need to plan ahead. For example, you might enjoy Baja California Sur in the winter, Cuenca, Ecuador, in the spring, San Miguel de Allende, Mexico, in the summer, and Las Palmas de Gran Canaria, Spain, in the fall.

LEARN THE LANGUAGE

I cannot emphasize this too strongly. The biggest single mistake expats make, no matter what country they move to, is to not learn at least the basic phrases in the language of their new home. Expats from the UK are the worst, but many Americans aren't far behind them. I once asked a world traveler from London, who'd lived in the Canary Islands for more that twenty years, why he had never taken a single lesson in the Spanish language.

"No need, old boy. If some clerk or agent does not understand me, I just step back, look around, and say in a loud, clear voice, 'Does . . . anyone . . . here . . . speak . . . *English?*'"

WHY CHOOSE SPANISH?

Well, for one reason, it is the language of Mexico, Central America, South America (except Brazil), and Spain—some of the prime places for setting up a new home. Further, I know of no language easier for an English-speaking person to learn. Do you know why there are no national spelling bees in Spanish-speaking countries? It's because words in Spanish are spelled exactly as they sound. Even kids can correctly spell words they hear for the first time. Therefore, be sure to learn phonetics at the very beginning, as we did when we moved to the Canary Islands. Within a few months I could read most anything out loud and my listeners could understand it, even if I could not!

BAJA CALIFORNIA SUR, MEXICO

Most of Baja California Sur is peaceful, far from the drug wars in the state of Sinaloa on the far side of the Sea of Cortez. My favorite small town is Loreto, on the inland coast (Sea of Cortez). It's a relatively clean town with a great airport (nonstop flights to/from Los Angeles) and a terrific marina just to the south. If you like deep-sea fishing, this is the place to keep your boat.

However, if you wish to be closer to the American big-box stores and/or an expat community, consider La Paz, the capital of Baja California Sur. This is a cultural center having a university, a theater, and a number of museums. The per capita income is among the highest in Mexico. North Americans have not yet overrun La Paz, although my guess is that there are several thousand expats here.

Winters in Baja California Sur are great, but the summers are hot. If you can't stand prolonged heat, head for:

SAN MIGUEL DE ALLENDE, GUANAJUATO

This small city (80,000) is in the central highlands of Mexico, between Leon and Querétaro. If you must have heating, air

conditioning, and a central location, then your rent will be similar to that in the United States. Prices drop dramatically when
you move to one of the small villages thirty to forty minutes
away from the city, but once again—few Americans are willing
to do this. (Our friends Alex and Laura are Mexican nationals
who spent seventeen years in the states before returning to Mexico last year and settling down in a village about a half-hour out
of San Miguel. They live in an old motorhome alongside a relatively new home they use as an office for an Internet business.
The rent is just $90 a month, but Alex himself admits it's a steal,
and it was very difficult to find.)

In San Miguel, you'll find Office Depot, Starbucks, Block-
buster, and McDonalds. In Celaya (forty-five minutes away) you
can visit Costco, Sam's Club, Walmart, and Home Depot. There
are some 10,000 part-time or full-time North American expats
in this small city—quite a number of them painters, sculptors,
and writers.

CUENCA, ECUADOR

Guayaquil, on the Pacific coast, is Ecuador's largest city, with a
population of 2.3 million and another 800,000 in the metro-
politan area, but do not move there—too big, too dirty, and too
much crime. Instead, check out Cuenca (population 350,000), a
much quieter, safer, and cleaner city up in the highlands. (The
September 2009 edition of *International Living*, named Cuenca
the world's number-one retirement destination, although it was
a bit of a puff piece.)

Days are generally warm the year round, but not hot. Nights
are cool enough so that sweaters or jackets are needed. Below is
an e-mail from Mark and Ruth, Spanish-speaking friends who
moved from Texas to Cuenca last year:

Living here is very nice. It's very peaceful. We never feel afraid. The buses only cost 25 cents. They also use a swipe card that works like a debit card. You pay $1.70 for the card and then load it with whatever you want, $1, $5, $10. Then you don't need change for the bus. The Ecuadorian embassy has info on retiring here. There are a lot of gringos moving/living here. Also, they are building new condos everywhere.

I asked Mark what he currently pays for their furnished apartment, and how much an upscale condo would cost, with a great view.

We pay $375 for a 2 bedroom/2 bath in a decent part of town (we pay our own utilities). Some of our local friends pay $300 or less. However, the majority of retired Americans here pay $500 or $600 a month. We looked at a beautiful condo yesterday. Called "Linda Vista," it had a great view of the city, price was $150,000. That was for a lower floor, the ones higher up were around $175,000. All were about 1,400 square feet.

As for medical expenses, Mark writes:

Most doctors here charge $25–35 for an office visit. An American neighbor of ours got her gall bladder ultrasound here and it cost 1/10 of what they wanted for that in the states. I got an abdomen scanned in Peru for $330 and in the states they wanted over $3,000.

Friends in Spain tell me that many Spaniards fly to Ecuador to get cosmetic surgery done here, as the work is said to be excellent and prices cheap.

Ecuador uses the U.S. dollar so no need to worry about calculating exchange rates. There are currently about 1,000 expats in Cuenca. The general consensus is that the cost of living is about half of what they paid in the United States, Canada, or the UK.

THE CANARY ISLANDS, SPAIN

In 1959, we left the Midwest and moved to the Canaries (two Spanish provinces off the coast of Morocco). At that time it was a great place to raise children. Under Generalissimo Francisco Franco, prices were low, girls were chaperoned until married, drugs were almost nonexistent, and my wife and daughters could walk the streets of Santa Cruz de Tenerife at midnight in perfect safety.

When Franco died in 1975, all that changed. Elections were held and the Socialists, desperate for votes, promised the young people they would not be punished for using small amounts of drugs. The Socialist Party won and all Spain was the loser. Near the end of 2011, however, the Socialists under José Zapatero were finally kicked out of office. Mariano Rajoy (People's Party) gained an absolute majority with 16 percentage points over the Socialists, so hopes are now for somewhat better times in the years ahead.

RENTS

Until the recent recession, rents were quite expensive. However, Spain has the same real estate problem as the United States, or worse. Sales have virtually stopped, and so owners of villas and apartments—unable to sell them—are renting them out at lower-than-normal rates. "It's better to have a little income," says one owner, "than nothing at all."

Friends in Puerto Rosario, Fuerteventura, report monthly rentals of two-bedroom apartments to have come down to the 300- to 400-euro range. This price range also applies to villages away from the main cities on most of the islands.

The Canaries enjoy a subtropical climate, with mild to warm temperatures throughout the year. Sunshine is abundant and it seldom rains. For this reason, villas and apartments often have neither heating nor air conditioning.

Medical and dental expenses are somewhat lower than in North America, although office calls are similar, usually about 80 euros.

LAS PALMAS DE GRAN CANARIA

This is a cosmopolitan city of about 400,000, with direct air connections to the main cities of Europe as well as to South Africa. The absolute best place to live in Las Palmas is in an apartment building overlooking Las Canteras, a beach as well-known in Europe as is Waikiki to North Americans. (Topless bathing here is common, as is the case with all beaches and hotel pools in the Canary Islands.) Apartment rentals along the boardwalk start at 750 euros, down from double that a few years ago. Not bad, considering the location and the beautiful view of sand and sea.

There are no North American expats here, but you will find small, well-established communities of German, British, Scandinavian, Russian, Chinese, Arabic, and African people living here.

CONCLUSION

Wherever you live, your country is not perfect, but neither is any other nation on the planet. If you plan a future move, the best advice I can give you is to first *visit* there, before you cut any ties with the states. Rent a modest apartment for three months. Check out the prices of everything from food to real estate. You may end up deciding that where you live right now isn't *that* bad after all.

27

INTERNATIONAL PRIVACY 101

In some countries, "international privacy" is an oxymoron. Consider Japan.

Japan has a registration system for all citizens *and foreigners* at the local city office. Citizens are registered pen-to-paper on family trees called *koseki*. This is the foundation for employment, bank accounts, national health insurance, voting. All of the aforementioned activities are cross-checked through the city office.

Says an American expat living in Japan:

For Japanese people, it is impossible to dodge this system. If there is any doubt raised as to your registration, you will find your bank account temporarily inactive, health insurance card not working at the clinic, etc. This happened to me several years ago. I moved and thought I would tell everybody later, as in thirty days or so. I went to the doctor for a checkup and the receptionist asked if I moved recently. I said yes. She wrote down my new address.

How did she know? My company's HR staff called me to say that my bank called to confirm my address before my salary could be deposited. My name didn't match the address on my salary deposit. How did they know? Landlords are expected to inform on tenants who come or go!

Japanese don't use checks. Instead, they go to any ATM and type in the recipient's name or company name, bank name, account number, and insert cash. A record is then sent to all parties. One's entire financial life is recorded—how much the telephone bill is, medical clinics visited, religious contributions, debts paid to loan sharks, consumer finance companies, etc.

> *Note:* When the first edition of *How to Be Invisible* was published in 2000, my agent had just one request from a foreign publisher. It was from Japan! I sold the rights, the book was published, and I have copies to prove it. I can only assume the publisher was left with a lot of unsold copies.

From this point on I will deal with a few specific countries. However, don't skip over them because advice for one country may well apply to another. Or, you may choose to travel to a specific country in order to open a bank account or pick up an untraceable cell phone.

UNITED KINGDOM

At first glance, the UK may seem to be not far removed from Japan. In fact, the UK is light-years ahead of Japan when it comes to surveillance by CCTV cameras.

Currently, the government is tracking and storing records of all international travel into and out of the UK. It records your name, address, telephone number, seat reservation, travel itinerary, and your credit card details. It keeps these for ten years.

According to an article in the November 4, 2011, *Daily Mail,* some 3 million snooping operations have been carried out among UK citizens since 2001. This includes 20,000 warrants for the interception of phone calls, e-mails, and Internet use. There have been nearly 3 million requests for communications data (phone bills, location data) and over 4,000 authorizations for intrusive surveillance—which usually means planting a bug in a citizen's home or car.

Although the UK and Ireland are part of the European Union (EU), they do not belong to the Schengen area. However, once they pass through the border controls into mainland Europe, they will be in the Schengen area.

> *Note to Americans:* In accordance with the Schengen Convention of June 14, 1985, the twenty-five Member States (all in Europe) have abolished checks on persons at the time of crossing of their internal borders. Hence the checks on persons are only carried out at the time of crossing of the external border of a Member State, which then acts on behalf of all of the other States of the Schengen area.

This means UK citizens can then freely travel—*and work*—all over Europe, with no more border controls. They are thus far from the UK's CCTV cameras and are often far from government scrutiny as well.

IRELAND

The following is from a reader in County Cork:

> There are a whole heap of us non-Americans out here, (I am Irish/British) who do not feel very included in your output. In the current volatile economic situation, a book on preserving

wealth would be a winner here in Europe. We have a shaky euro, pound, etc., and are scared to convert to dollars.

I suggested putting some of his euros into gold, and received this answer:

A small number of outlets who sell gold and silver will not deal for cash, but require one to pay by bank draft or debit. It is rumored that they have been leaned on by big brother. They just want to be paid through your bank and they want to arrange delivery to your home! I don't want big brother or anyone else calling around to see how my gold bars are getting on!

If this is the case in your own country as well, you might consider traveling to another country—both Hong Kong and the United States come to mind—where anonymous purchases of gold are allowed. Another option is to travel to Canada and open a bank account in Canadian dollars (which I consider to be more stable than the American dollar). Tens of thousands of Americans already have Canadian accounts, as do thousands more from around the world.

Not ready to travel? No problem. Just start accumulating Canadian currency. Easy to do in any land where Canadians visit, which means most anywhere in the world.

SPAIN

In many ways, Spain is no better and no worse than many other countries in the European Union, with one exception. On March 11, 2004, ten bombs were detonated on trains arriving at Atocha, Madrid's main train station. Cell phones had been used to detonate the bombs. From that date forward, it has been almost impossible to obtain a cell phone in Spain without proving your identity. However, things are not quite that tight elsewhere.

SWEDEN

Unlike some of the EU countries, I'd heard that anonymous cell phones might be available in Sweden. I checked with a friend there; below is his reply:

> I myself have four "burner phones," which I use frequently when buying/selling stuff on the Swedish equivalent of Craigslist (blocket.se). They are bought with cash and so is the cell phone card (which has your phone number) that you need to operate the phone.
>
> At no point am I obliged to identify myself to anyone when buying and/or using a prepaid cell phone card. However, if I want to get 100–200 SEK "for free" as a prepaid voucher I can register my prepaid cell phone card. Most people do this, but I never do.
>
> It is not mandatory to register or identify yourself while using prepaid services. However, having a "subscription" does require registration. Most people have subscriptions since this simplifies your bills and you always "have credit" on your phone since you pay *after* you have used the phone for a month.
>
> Last, but not least, the prepaid MasterCards (spendon.se, use Google translation to read it) can be used to add credits to your prepaid cell phone card through the Internet, so you can get someone else to buy your phone and SIM card for you, as well as the prepaid MasterCard and then just go to the library, use their free computers and add credit to your phone later on.

BELGIUM

The following are two questions I posed to a reader in Belgium, and his answers:

Does the government know where you actually live? If so, could that be avoided?

In my case, yes, the government knows where I live, but this could certainly be avoided if someone wanted to. Many people over here use street addresses as a mail drop without actually living there in exchange for a monthly fee to the owner who provides such a service.

The only negative with this is that a local police agent comes to pay a visit to see if you actually live there. Most people can make an appointment with this officer to meet at the mail drop address on a certain date and hour, so in fact this is a minor inconvenience and the officer only pays a one-time visit.

Can you get a cell phone without showing photo ID?

Yes. Of course, the stores ask to register them, but you can give any fake name and address you want. Nothing is checked. We can also buy prepaid cell phone cards without showing any ID nor even register them. I have about five new cell phone SIM cards in my home to change my number if necessary or appropriate. In conclusion, if you keep a low profile, privacy is certainly doable in Belgium.

MEXICO

I sent the following questions to a friend in La Paz, Baja California Sur, who has lived in Mexico for eleven years, and below are his replies.

Does the government know where you actually live? If so, could that be avoided?

If you own property, they would know where you live as everything is tied to your passport and visa. If you rent a place, normally the bills are in the name of the owner of the property, and so you just take a recent bill in "comprobante de domicilio" in as proof-of-living address. This is if you want to set up a bank account, or for some government office such as Immigration, etc.

Can you get a cell phone without showing photo ID?

It used to be that you could, but now due to all of the narco problems throughout Mexico, they require you to show a passport, which is tied to the telephone number. Of course, there are always ways to get around things like this such as having the phone in the name of a business or under someone else's name and you just pay it.

Could mail from the United States be received in a company name or a fake name?

Yes, I think you could do that without much of a problem. You can either use the normal Mexican mail system (which I like to call "Burro Express" because it takes so long), or you can rent a box and they ship your U.S. mail to the private box. Several companies offer this paid for service.

Any other comments on privacy—or lack of it—in Mexico?

Mexico is a country that *loves* bureaucracy and red tape! To do anything here you must have piles of paperwork and everything in two or three copies. I don't know where they store all the piles of paperwork that is required to do things such as Immigration, Hacienda (tax entity), to open a bank account, or virtually anything else. They are now beginning to develop systems that are electronically based, but it's a long way away from being simple. Of course, there is corruption here just like in all countries but not nearly as much as there used to be when I first moved to Mexico eleven years ago. In the past, you couldn't get a visa unless you paid two or three people under the table, but now that the government has cracked down on that, the only way for that to happen is if you pal up with somebody who is in a higher position on the inside. It's all about connections: Who you know!

SWITZERLAND

I asked a world-traveling correspondent who flies in and out of Switzerland the following questions, and below are his replies.

Are you allowed to not use socialized medicine, and just pay the bills yourself and perhaps even use another name? Or must you always have to prove your identity?

This depends on the country. In the UK it will be [George Orwell's] *1984* very soon. I have, in the past when I was an illegal immigrant, set up a company in Switzerland, which paid my medical. But in Switzerland the insurance is private, but mandatory. So I must have proof of this and this must be recorded by the government. All insurance in Europe is mandatory I believe. If you cannot afford the CHF320 per month for private insurance, then you must take socialized medicine. But you have to prove to the government of the country you live in that you are insured. Same for Australia. I live in Perth three months out of the year, to keep from freezing to death, and when you wish to live in this country with any visa other than a tourist visa then you need proof of insurance or they give it to you socialized. Identity is always needed. You can use another name, but you need identity for this as well.

Solution: Set up an AG in Switzerland, hire yourself as a foreign consultant, and register the new name under the company's insurance. They will cover you anywhere in the world and reimburse you.

Note: "AG" stands for *Aktiengesellschaft*, a corporation, which is owned by shareholders. The term is used in Germany, Austria, and Switzerland.

***Could you fly to a country outside of the European Union
(EU) and get medical help by paying cash and not revealing
your identity?***

Yes, many people do this. Mainly Thailand for dental. It's not
close, but the world is small and these flights are easy to find. But
if in your country insurance is *mandatory*, then is it worth it? You
cannot legally reside in Europe with no insurance. However, as I
said, you can register your insurance in Switzerland if you can set
up an AG, hire yourself as a consultant (getting your permission
B), and then pay the bills through the AG's bank accounts.

What about banking?

Privacy is what Switzerland is special for. Even though it has
mandatory laws the reality is you can keep a bank account private here. Every Swiss person has two bank accounts. He tells
no one about his second (secret) account. The Swiss government
cannot touch this or ask about tax or anything. (Typically at a
Raiffeisen Bank, not even the Raiff Bank in the next stadt [can-
ton] knows who you are. Someone would have to find your
bank, not easy, then have to find out how to get your information from the bank. If someone finds your Raiff Bank card they
can say "*Ha*, got you!" But there is no way to find the amount in
the account, unless they find the *exact* bank you use—and even
then—can somehow get to this data.)

***Can you have some address other than where you really
live, on your insurance card? If not, what about people who
have more than one home, such as those who live in the Canaries in winter and Switzerland in the summer?***

Yes, this is possible. But you must show that your address is being lived in (bedroom, closets with your possessions, kitchen,
etc.). This address cannot be a friend's home. They ask for your
rental agreement and come to visit. A couple of Serbian basket-

ball players in Switzerland were asked to leave the country for this reason. So if you have a second address, you must make sure the place is livable. Then you can reside in a different place.

Can't you move, say, to Spain but still maintain everything (including an insurance card) with your Swiss address? And just be "visiting" in Spain?

Yes, this would be the best-case scenario. My boss lives in Spain, but has the company in BVI with banking and insurance in Switzerland. It's easy from the Swiss side, but harder from the Spanish side, unless you do not wish to spend much money in Spain. Visible signs of wealth can be visible signs of stupidity. Gets you into trouble.

PERU

Many third world countries operate on bribes, as did Spain under Generalissimo Franco. If you have enough money, you can often operate in relative obscurity. Peru might not be thought of as "third world" but I wrote to David, an American who lives in a small coastal village in Peru. Below are the six questions I asked him, and his answers.

Does Peru operate on the basis of bribes, as was the case when we moved to the Canary Islands in 1959? If so, with bribes, could you get by with another name and a false resident permit?

Yes, bribes are fairly common. Not far north of here is a checkpoint for contraband coming in from Ecuador, and Linda and I had gone to a beach north of there. On the way back, the taxi van stopped there and the driver didn't want to have to pull all the stuff stowed under the tarp on top. So he slipped the guys a bill, and they let him go. They did make sure the captain couldn't see them do it, though. I don't have any idea how widespread it is since we haven't had to do much paperwork ourselves.

Are there spot checks on any roads, where you have to "show papers"?

I can't speak for private vehicles since we use public transportation. Of course, at the border crossings you do. I'm sure private vehicles traveling any distance will sooner or later have to stop at a checkpoint.

Does the government know where you actually live? If so, could that be avoided?

The government doesn't keep track of where we live unless there is some need for them to know. Enforcement is very loose here, so I doubt they know where most people live.

Can you get a cell phone without showing photo ID?

Yes.

Could you get mail from the United States in a company name or a fake name?

Yes, not a problem.

Any other comments on privacy—or lack of it—in Peru?

I don't think most people know what privacy is here. First of all, no one tells the people what the laws are. Second, no one enforces them unless there is a good reason (usually money to be squeezed). Again, I think you could live under an assumed name. But you would have to deal with border crossings where they must see your passport and visa up to date, either at the airport or the border checkpoints. That system is computerized and linked to Interpol. A person could probably come to Peru on a tourist visa and lose themselves here pretty easily.

CONCLUSIONS REGARDING INTERNATIONAL PRIVACY

Almost all governments make every possible effort to know who you are, where you live, what you buy on credit, what you owe, and how much you have in the bank. Your job is to make every possible effort to hide this information. This includes, but is not limited to:

HIDING YOUR HOME ADDRESS

In many countries, what you say is your home address will be checked out. One way to avoid this, once you have been checked, is to move. Another is to say you live with your parents or a relative, but in this case they have to back you up. A third way, too expensive for most, is to keep two separate living quarters, one your official residence, and the other where you actually sleep at night.

However, even though your home address may show up on your National Identity Card and/or your driver's license, why let anyone other than close friends ever know where you actually live? When ID must be shown, just use your passport. (If you do not yet have a passport, by all means get one because passports normally do not show your home address.)

In the mid-1960s I was the leading commercial photographer in Spain's province of Santa Cruz de Tenerife, and the first one to work with large photo murals to decorate hotels, restaurants, colleges, and the private offices of dentists, doctors, and architects. As such, I often met with clients on a friendly basis in coffee shops in Santa Cruz. I was welcome at any time in their offices, but never, never in their homes. In fact, I had no idea where any of them lived. Many were millionaires. (The typical millionaire might live in a gorgeous home hidden among landscaping that took in an entire square block, but all you could see from the outside was a ten-foot wall topped with broken glass.) I suggest you imitate them by never giving out your home address to any-one not entitled to it. Do not list it in the phone book nor on your business cards. Never have anything delivered to your home ad-dress—no mail, no UPS, no DHL, no FedEx, *nada en absoluto.*

IF YOU ARE BEING TRACKED . . .

Thus far, the information about various countries has been for those of you who merely wish to keep your private information private. If someone has set a private investigator after you, and if this PI has unlimited funds, then the danger point is when he discovers which hotel you are in. He will bribe someone—often a clerk at the front desk—into answering questions, such as:

"What information did he fill out when he signed in? What vehicle is he driving? How did he pay? Was anyone else in the lobby with him when he signed in? What was charged to the room? Which movies is he watching? What was taken from the minibar? Any special requests made for that room?"

He will then contact the maid who is scheduled to make up your room. For as little as $20 he may be allowed access to what-ever you've tossed into a wastebasket. If you are out late at night, the PI may even show up during your absence. He'll wave a dummy subpoena in front of the bored night manager and de-mand the key to your room. If that happens, let's hope that you've put your laptop computer and any sensitive documents into your room's safe.

THE REMEDY

Plan ahead to stay with a friend. Or check out Craigslist for rooms to rent. If all else fails, find someone who will allow you to sleep on a couch. Check out www.couchsurfing.com, www.globalfree loaders.com, or www.place2stay.net. One of the biggest is Hospitality Club (www.hospitalityclub.org), founded in 2000 by Veit Kuehne, from Dusseldorf, Germany. Start there first.

If you suspect you are being followed from the airport, make sure to lose any tail before heading for your destination. Or, for a more permanent solution, rent a small motor home and sleep in it at night.

THE UNITED STATES OF AMERICA

To totally disappear from the radar, consider heading for "the land of the free" and disappearing into the 11 million undocumented immigrants already there!

A SAD STORY, A SECRET, AND A FEW PREDICTIONS

As I prepare to send my finished manuscript to St. Martin's Press, some especially interesting e-mails are coming in from readers. Below is one I just received this morning, from a client who's just set up a ghost address in Alaska. This is the kind of story you just can't make up.

Don't just skim through it, please. Take your time. See if you can figure out what (if anything) he did wrong, and what (if anything) he could have done to avoid this sad tale. *What follows is verbatim.* I hereby certify and declare that I have not changed the punctuation, syntax, nor a single word, not even those that are misspelled.

IN ARTHUR'S OWN WORDS

I am one of the cleanest guys around and was a boy scout. I only got two speeding tickets in my life and that is it as far as breaking the law. I have been so careful all my life with obeying the law and also very careful at avoiding bad people especially bad women. I have turned away many many women in my travels. I strongly believe in law and order and catching and punishing those that don't obey the law.

I learned Spanish and started to travel to Latin America where I have met very good and morale women more so than many Americans. I have visited many women and their families in Latin America. They are very sincere and very respectful. I guess I started to let my guard down because I came across a woman who is a compulsive liar. I even tried to end the relationship at one point but she was so dominant and she begged me not to. She lied with such strong conviction that she herself appeared to believe in everything she said and would say it with authority.

I, being an engineer, traditionally base all of my decisions on evidence and I always ask probing questions but this women countered every one of my questions with answers and stories. She was the one in a million that could successfully deceive me and did. She told me that she was a medical doctor working for the Brazilian Navy but for the moment was under contract with a clinic in Peru. She told me about how wonderful the benefits are from the government from Brazil for mothers including single mothers.

She also told me she wanted to marry, leave the Navy, and receive the wonderful pension that the brazilian navy owes her. Every week she told me stories about her job and the politics at the clinic.

We had a relationship for 6 months. The first time I met her she introduced me to her "mother" and her niece and nephew in Peru. I have their face book pages bookmarked. They spoke portuguese so I could not converse with them like I wanted to because I speak Spanish. Also there were

I think at least two other women that communicated with me supporting her lies. I was ganged up on in an elaborate fraudulent manner.

Months later she told me that she is pregnant. I demanded her to show me ID. She sent me photos of various ID cards. I asked her about each an every one of them . . . what is each ID card called and what is it used for? etc. I suffered for weeks trying to request help from the Brazilian consolate to confirm for me that her IDs are real. They refused to help me telling me that they don't offer such a service. The woman then told me that the Brazilian Navy has changed its rules and regulations, has taken away her benefits and her pension until she gets married and the marriage would have to take place within 5 months from the date of the letter. She sent me photos of the letter. She started to create medical emergencies every week with demands for my money since she no longer had a salary and benefits.

I lost $9000 dollars until I was able to find a company in Florida that specializes in investigating Brazilians. This company confirmed for me that all her IDs including Brazilian government IDs with "Marinha Do Brasil" on them are false. I have reported everything to the US Embassy in Lima, Brasilia, and to the Brazilian consolate in Washington DC.

To this day the woman and/or accomplices sends me threats at this email address. Although she has been proven wrong in so many things, she clings to being pregnant and does not apologize for anything. During the coarse of all this she has made many threats including suicide, threats of having copied my passport, threats of having intimate photos of me, threats of sending the photos to my employers, threats of abuse or rape and now threats of creating a legal case against me in USA. If she were to be pregnant the twins would be born in early December. She also has all the while said that she has a twin sister but I always doubted that and I doubted the photos she had with her supposed twin sister. She was using the twin sister as her way out of the crime with me and I have caught her.

When I learned that her photos of her IDs were false, I told her that she is a criminal for committing fraud with me and also for sending fotos of false government issued IDs from the government of Brazil. She is a devil. She was sending me 30 text messages a day at one time and sending so many emails declaring lies with conviction to put pressure on me to send her more money for some new made up medical emergency. She even sent me an echograph of the two fetuses. I have learned that this too is easy to falsify. I did have a video chat wth her at the 3 month mark but I don't know if she was just fat or pregnant. IF pregnant who knows if she still is and if it is mine. Too many unknowns.

I have changed my phone numbers and moved my residence. I have invested a great deal of time now into removing my information from the public on the internet but this takes a long time so I have to assume that she knows where I work and where my parents live. I am sitting tight and praying that December and January will pass without any event.

This woman is a criminal and lies with such strong conviction and dominance that it is apparent to me now that this was her full time job whether she is part of a group of women or a group of women under a pimp in Iqtuitos, Peru and that she has a long experience at success at this. That is the source of her conviction and dominant personality. I became blind in just looking at the resume of a

woman instead of forcefully demanding the evidence because for me it is easy to meet a pretty woman but it is
difficult to meet a professional woman that is at least attractive with my views. I am so picky and careful . . . this
is really a one in a million situation that has happened to
me but it HAPPENED.

I now realize how open USA is and how dangerous it is
to my well being and my family's well being. I also now realize that although I was always asking the questions, I was
lacking the strength to put my foot down and demand forc-
fully to see evidence or WALK AWAY IMMEDIATELY
when confronting such a dominant woman.

I have to now learn the process of buying a home under
a trust or LLC.

—Arthur

SO WHAT DO YOU THINK, DEAR READER?

Was the woman's story too good to be true? If you were Arthur,
what would you do now? If you are one of those rare people who
believe the entire Bible to be true, then you will see his mistakes, but what was the very first one? Otherwise, at what later
point would you have first had some doubts?

Arthur makes no mention of the moral issue, so I will leave
that aside. Further, hindsight is so much better than foresight
that it is difficult to say that Arthur acted naïvely.

"There but for the grace of God . . ."

HOW TO PROTECT YOURSELF IN THE FUTURE

You may be happily married, but what about your sisters or broth-
ers, your nieces or nephews, or even your kids? There are lessons
here for us all, and not just as to dating. Think about these things

when making new friends, joining a club, or considering a partner in business. Let's assume you're a young man in the market for a bride. You've just met Brenda, and lightning has struck. Now what?

- Get her true name but withhold or disguise your own.
- Google her name. Ask around. See who else knows her, and what they say about her.
- Find out where she works. If it's a public place, stop by and see if she's really there. If so, have a chat with one of her coworkers or superiors.
- Get her address if you can, and google that. Withhold or disguise your own address and place of work.

Instead of a phone number, trade e-mail addresses with Brenda. Yours, Joe, will be a one-off—used for no other purpose. Hers you can google. In fact, if she had some pet phrase, you might even google that, to see if she's saying the very same thing to other men. (Some predators have been exposed in just that way!)

In fact, if you are currently playing the field, do as a certain flight attendant does, who flies on international runs. She disguises her true name and keeps in touch via e-mail with seven male friends in various countries. Each one has been given a Yahoo! e-mail address that is unique to this person alone. Any time she wants to cut off communication, all she has to do is close that specific account.

¡Adios, amigo!

THE MORAL OF ARTHUR'S STORY

Don't think something similar can't ever happen to you. Since this book was first published in 2000, I have received more e-mails than I can remember, that started out, "You know, I never thought this could happen to me, but . . ."

A SECRET REVEALED

None of the information in this book will be of assistance to you unless you put the suggestions into practice. Do not wait until you can find the time—you may never find it. Do not wait until you can "do it right," because that day may never come.

All successful persons can list one or more secrets for their success. My entrepreneurial father passed on his own two secrets of success to me when I left home to seek my way in the world. ("To make money, you must go where the money is," and "Never take a partner.") Earl Nightingale wrote an entire best-selling book with a single theme, *The Strangest Secret*. ("We become what we think about.")

Well, *my* secret isn't very strange. In fact, it's so obvious that I fear you will disregard it:

> **For every desired action, set a date, and when the date arrives, just go ahead and do it, *NO MATTER WHAT.***

My secret rule has no rhyme to it, but it works for me and it will work for you. Make a list of what you wish to accomplish and *set a date* to complete each item. Your goal is to never again allow any strangers to have your home address. Below are a few goals to consider:

- Obtain at least one new address and give this to your out-of-town relatives, friends, banks, insurance companies, utility companies, IRS, DMV, and everyone else.

- Disconnect your present telephone. Then have it reconnected in another name. Add a prepaid cell phone as well.

- Order—or prepare on the computer—new checks for your bank account that will show neither your full name nor your address. Start with a high number.

- For sensitive e-mail, use one of the Web-based accounts

such as Yahoo! or Gmail. Use discernment when filling in the "personal" information.

- If you are renting, move. If you are a homeowner, sell, then start over.
- Order one or more LLCs so they will be on hand when you suddenly need them.
- Start an invisible home-based business if you have not already done so.
- Look at every challenge to your privacy as an adventure. Get a life, have fun during the day, sleep without worries at night.

As this book goes to press, it is as up-to-date as I can make it. However, some changes may have taken place before you have this book in your hands. Check www.howtobeinvisible.com for any updated information.

A FEW PREDICTIONS

"Widespread police surveillance," writes author Bruce Schneier, "is the very definition of a police state . . . A future in which privacy would face constant assault was so alien to the framers of the Constitution that it never occurred to them to call out privacy as an explicit right. Of course being watched in your own home was unreasonable. Watching at all was an act so unseemly as to be inconceivable among gentlemen in their day."

We aren't to the police state quite yet, but we are heading in that direction. As for future dangers, here are a few predictions:

- The dangers of being on *any* social network will increase.
- The dangers of having your e-mail read by strangers will increase.

- Sexting and sextortion will increase.
- Driver's licenses will turn into national ID cards.
- The powers of both local police and federal agents will increase.
- The chance of having your computer and your smartphone searched will increase.
- Unrest and riots such as the "Arab Spring" will come to both the United States and Europe.
- Terrorism will increase, and somewhere a plane will be brought down by a shoulder-fired rocket.
- No matter where you live, more and more CCTVs and other cameras will be put in place.
- The Puritan work ethic will continue to decrease in popularity. An increasing number of young people will expect the government to take money from the rich and give it to them, with no sacrifice or hard work on their part.

To keep up with the rapid changes in how to be invisible, sign up for my e-mail alerts and regularly check my Web site and blog. Since this book was first published, tens of thousands of readers have successfully faded from view. So can you.

Yours faithfully,

JJ Luna

Las Palmas de Gran Canaria
April 2012

APPENDIX

CONTACTS

J.J. LUNA

Please contact me for information about ghost addresses in Alaska and in Spain's Canary Islands. I am also available for private consultations, usually in Bellevue, Washington, or in Las Vegas, Nevada. (No consultations by e-mail or telephone. If I am to help you, we need to talk one-on-one.)

Fairbanks, Alaska: Two addresses are provided, a street address and a PO box number. You may use either or both. This address is ideal for any LLC that is used to own real estate, vehicles (in most states), and as your personal address for low-profile bank accounts.

Arrecife de Lanzarote, Spain: Addresses here are available for (1) normal private mail, (2) domain name registration, and (3) an address that includes document storage to demonstrate legally that your "principal place of business" is indeed in Spain.

E-books: These currently include information about low-profile banking, living off the grid, surviving financial disasters, solid reasons for skipping college, and instructions about selecting a business for yourself and starting on the proverbial shoestring. By the time you read this, there may be further e-books on airline travel tips, selecting a safe house, and/or detailed information about moving to Mexico, Ecuador, or Spain's Canary Islands.

E-mail:	jack@jjluna.com
Web sites:	www.howtobeinvisible.com
	http://canaryislandspress.com
Blog:	http://blog.invisible-privacy.com

JOHN CLARK, ESQ.

John is one of the few attorneys I trust for privacy matters. Although he takes on very few "retainer clients," he offers fixed-fee privacy packages to anyone wishing to use trusts, LLCs, or both to protect privacy. He is a practicing California attorney specializing in the privacy challenges faced by California residents. For residents of other states, John can assist with document preparation or associate with local legal counsel for privacy seekers requiring hands-on help.

Web site:	www.privacylawoffice.com

R. ENRÍQUEZ SANCHEZ

Rosie Enríquez formed Nevada and Wyoming corporations for my European clients from 1989–1995. Since that time she has formed thousands of New Mexico limited liability companies for my clients worldwide. Hers is the only service I recommend and use personally. She keeps an inventory of preformed "shelf LLCs" on hand at all times for the ultimate in privacy and fast turnaround. Rosie can also form a "custom LLC" with any name you choose that is acceptable to the State of New Mexico, but please be patient—New Mexico can take several weeks or more to process paperwork. For further information:

Web site:	www.senoritarosie.com
E-mail:	rosie@senoritarosie.com

TIM LATRASSE

Tim is the Manager and Senior Investigator for Parker Lakes & Associates Investigative Services in California (CA PI#22954). He provides boutique confidential services and consults on matters of security and investigations with high net-worth individuals and various corporate entities, domestically and across the globe. In my opinion, he is one of the best in the business. Even more important, he's a straight shooter. I trust Tim implicitly. (*Note*: Sometimes it's best for your legal team to be the ones to request his services.)

Telephone: 1-866-660-1212

ONLINE NEWSLETTERS

KIM KOMANDO

Kim's daily newsletter deals with a vast variety of digital and electronic information. I always scroll down to "News of the Day" to see what's new—especially in regards to Internet dangers.

Web site: www.komando.com

SIMON BLACK

"I'm a student of the world," says Simon, "and I believe that travel is the greatest teacher. My knowledge is practical, and hopefully of significant use to you. Off the top of my head I could quote you the price of beachfront property in Croatia, where to bank in Dubai, the best place to store gold in Singapore, which cities in Mexico are the safest, which hospitals in Asia are the most cost effective, and how to find condo foreclosure listings in Panama."

Although that sounds like a puff piece, I have come to believe that Simon is the real thing. His daily newsletters are for those of you in a narrow niche: either you wish to move to a foreign country (preferably Chile, where he has a land development project) or you wish to invest or bank in another country. If nothing else, his comments on the current world situation are enlightening!

Web site: www.sovereignman.com

BOOKS ABOUT PRIVACY

FRANK AHEARN

Frank's book *How to Disappear* is not for everyone. However, if you feel that my chapter 24 ("How to Disappear and Never Be Found") applies to your present circumstances, then you may find Frank's information on that subject to be of additional help. I was pleased to see him recommend *How to Be Invisible* on page 51 of his book, but displeased at his gratuitous use of the f-word.

MARK NESTMANN

Mark is a lawyer and writes like a lawyer. However, if you want a reference work of infinite detail on every aspect of privacy, at home or abroad, then I recommend his *Lifeboat* series (three volumes) without reservation. When it comes to the nuts-and-bolts details of privacy, LLCs, and offshore information, Mark's books stand alone. For example, he lists "28 strategies to prevent identity theft, 11 ways to achieve 'residential anonymity,' 19 ways trusts protect privacy and wealth, 22 tactics to audit-proof your tax return," and "The 11 countries best suited for wealth preservation."

For details, go to http://nestmann.com/the-lifeboat-strategy -to-financial-security/?affid=2. Then check my Web site for recommended books, because I sometimes talk Mark into allowing a fifteen-minute free consultation if the *Lifeboat* volumes are ordered due to my recommendation.

BOOKS THAT EXPLAIN THE DANGERS OF SOCIAL NETWORKING

KEVIN MITNICK

Kevin Mitnick needs no introduction. If you run a business with employees and think you are protected, Kevin's books will disabuse you of that notion. Highly entertaining, as well!

> *Ghost in the Wires: My Adventures as the World's Most Wanted Hacker*
>
> *The Art of Deception: Controlling the Human Element of Security*
>
> *The Art of Intrusion: The Real Stories Behind the Exploits of Hackers, Intruders and Deceivers*

CHRISTOPHER HADNAGY

Christopher, author of *Social Engineering: The Art of Human Hacking*, has been involved with computers and technology for over fifteen years. Although his book is not as entertaining as the Mitnick books, you will discover just what it takes to excel as a social engineer. (It's always good to know your enemy.)

CONTACTS FOR STALKING VICTIMS

BETH GIVENS

Beth is the director of Privacy Rights Clearinghouse in San Diego, California. In early 2000, *Playboy* editor Chip Rowe contacted

Beth to ask if she knew of any author who was an expert in the field of privacy. She kindly referred him to me. This was the first I'd heard of her, but not the last. (I wrote the article for *Playboy*, and it was published as "The Invisible Man Lying Low in the Global Village." That article sold thousands of *How to Be Invisible* books!) The Privacy Rights Clearinghouse has a vast amount of information on privacy, but the section of most interest is "Fact Sheet 14: Are You Being Stalked?"

Web page: www.privacyrights.org/fs/fs14-stk.htm

JUDIE DILDAY

Judie is the president of End Stalking in America, Inc., in Chandler, Arizona. I first met her at one of the Los Angeles Police Department's annual Threat Management Conferences in Anaheim, California. (Always great information in these meetings about stalkers and stalking!) The purpose of her organization is "to be of assistance to all potential victims of stalking, and to assist those victims who are currently being harassed and stalked."

"End Stalking in America," she says, "provides direct and immediate one-on-one assistance to potential or current stalking victims. Each individual case is closely monitored daily from the initial onset of the harassment or stalking, though the judicial hearings, prosecution, while the offender is incarcerated, and after the offender is released from jail or prison. We work directly with the victim, law enforcement, and the judicial system."

Web site: www.esia.net

INDEX